Summer Success®

Math

Andy Clark • Patsy F. Kanter

GReaT S*uRCe®
EDUCATION GROUP
A Division of Houghton Mifflin Company

CREDITS

Writing: Sherrill Bennington, Jeanne Goldman, Tabula Rasa Publishing

Design/Production: Taurins Design

Illustration: Debra Spina Dixon

Cover and Package Design: Kristen Davis/Great Source

Printed in the United States of America

Great Source® and *Summer Success®* are registered trademarks of Houghton Mifflin Company.

International Standard Book Number–13: 978-0-669-53682-9

International Standard Book Number–10: 0–669–53682–2

1 2 3 4 5 6 7 8 9 10 MZ 11 10 09 08 07 06

Visit our web site: http://www.greatsource.com/

Name _____

NUMBER

Choose the best answer or write a response for each question.

1. What is another way to write $\frac{1}{2}$ as a percent?

   (A) 5%

   (B) 0.5%

   (C) 5.0%

   (D) 50%

2. Write $\frac{2}{3}$ as a decimal.

   (A) $0.\overline{3}$

   (B) 0.66

   (C) $0.\overline{6}$

   (D) 0.67

3. What is the opposite of 5?

   (A) −5

   (B) 0

   (C) 5

   (D) 10

4. What is the prime factorization of 24?

   (A) 6×4

   (B) $2 \times 2 \times 2 \times 3$

   (C) $2 \times 2 \times 6$

   (D) $4 \times 2 \times 3$

5. Fill in the table of values for $y = 5x + 20$.

x	y
0	
1	
2	
3	

6. Which number does **not** have the same value as the others?

   (A) 2,400,000

   (B) 2.4×10^6

   (C) $2.4 + 10^6$

   (D) 2 million, 400 thousand

OPERATIONS

7. What is $\frac{1}{2}$ of $\frac{1}{4}$?

(A) $\frac{3}{4}$

(B) $\frac{1}{2}$

(C) $\frac{1}{4}$

(D) $\frac{1}{8}$

8. What is $\frac{3}{4} - \frac{1}{3}$?

(A) 2

(B) $\frac{1}{2}$

(C) $\frac{5}{12}$

(D) $\frac{1}{4}$

9. Select the number line that shows the expression:

$$-3 + (-3)$$

(A)

(B)

(C)

(D)

10. What is the value of $2^3 \times 3$?

(A) 24

(B) 18

(C) 12

(D) 6

11. What is the value of x if $3x + 4 = 10$?

(A) 6

(B) $4\frac{2}{3}$

(C) 2

(D) 1

12. What is $-\frac{1}{3} \times \frac{1}{4}$?

(A) $\frac{7}{12}$

(B) $\frac{1}{12}$

(C) $-\frac{1}{12}$

(D) $-\frac{7}{12}$

PATTERNS AND ALGEBRA

13. Continue the pattern.

0.25, 0.75, 1.25, 1.75, 2.25,

_____, _____, _____

14. What is the value of term 12 for this pattern?

$\frac{5}{6}$, $1\frac{2}{3}$, $2\frac{1}{2}$, $3\frac{1}{3}$, . . .

(A)　$4\frac{1}{6}$

(B)　9

(C)　10

(D)　12

15. What is the value of the expression?

$$-3 \times (-8) \times (-1)$$

(A)　24

(B)　−24

(C)　−13

(D)　not given

16. Continue the pattern.

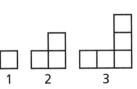

| 1 | 2 | 3 | 4 |

Figure	**Perimeter**
1	
2	
3	
4	

17. If $3a = 2.1$ and $a + b = 1.1$, what is the value of b?

(A)　0.4

(B)　0.7

(C)　1.1

(D)　2.1

18. One moon weighs as much as how many stars?

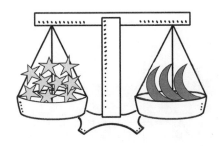

(A)　1

(B)　2

(C)　3

(D)　4

GEOMETRY AND MEASUREMENT

19. Which regular polygon has 4 lines of symmetry?

A

B

C

D

20. What is the measure of angle *ABC*?

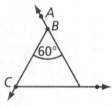

A 180°

B 120°

C 90°

D 60°

21. Plot the points and connect them in order.
(0, 5), (3, 0), (0, −5), (−3, 0), (0, 5)

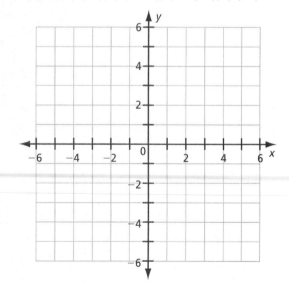

22. Which diagram shows a circle with a central angle?

A

B

C

D

Use the cube to answer problems 23–24.

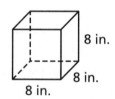

8 in.

8 in.

8 in.

23. Find the surface area of the cube.

A 64 in.²

B 256 in.²

C 384 in.²

D 512 in.²

24. Find the volume of the cube.

A 64 in.³

B 256 in.³

C 384 in.³

D 512 in.³

Name _____

DATA

Use the data for problems 25–27.

Small Pets

Animal	Average Life Span (years)	Average Litter Size
Gerbil	2.5	5.5
Guinea Pig	3.5	3.5
Hamster	2.5	7.5
Mouse	2.5	11
Rabbit	7.5	7
Rat	3.5	9

Adapted from greenapple.com

25. Make a scatter plot.

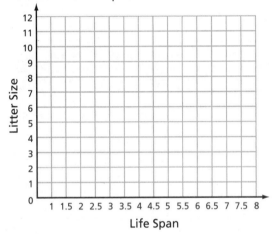

26. Is there a correlation between average life span and average litter size for these small pets? _____

27. Show the life span data on a stem-and-leaf plot.

Small Animal Life Span

Stems	Leaves

Key _____

Use the data for problems 28–30.

Coin Toss Results	
Heads	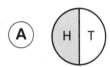
Tails	

28. Which circle graph **best** represents the results of the coin toss?

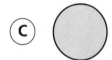

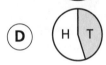

29. Explain why a line graph would not be appropriate to display the coin toss results.

_____

_____

_____

30. What is the theoretical probability of tossing heads?

(A) $\frac{2}{1}$

(B) $\frac{23}{17}$

(C) $\frac{17}{23}$

(D) $\frac{1}{2}$

PROBLEM SOLVING

Show your work.

31. Together, Jan and Dean have $28. Jan has $\frac{3}{4}$ as much money as Dean does.

How much does Jan have? _____

How much does Dean have? _____

32. In the following equations, each letter stands for a different integer.
What integer does each letter stand for?

$a + b = b$

$b + b = -6$

$a - c = 5$

$a =$ _____

$b =$ _____

$c =$ _____

Name _____

NUMBER AND OPERATIONS

Shade each model to show $\frac{1}{2}$. ◄1–3. MOC 028

1.

2. ◯◯◯◯◯◯

3.

Complete the ratio table. ◄4. MOC 036

4.

1	3		5
2		8	

Write the number. ◄5–7. MOC 036, 044, 442

5. $\frac{1}{2}$ as a decimal: _____

6. $\frac{1}{2}$ as a percent: _____

7. $\frac{1}{2} = \frac{?}{20}$ _____

PATTERNS AND ALGEBRA

Continue the pattern and answer the related questions. ◄8–10. MOC 104

8. $\frac{1}{2}$, 1, $1\frac{1}{2}$, 2, _____, _____, _____

9. If the pattern above continues, what is the tenth term? _____

10. Describe the rule for the pattern.

_____

_____

GEOMETRY AND MEASUREMENT

Draw the shape then answer the related question. ◄11–12. MOC 363, 365

11. Draw and label a rectangle whose length is 6 units. Its width is $\frac{1}{2}$ of its length.

12. Your answer to problem 11 is a scale drawing of a rectangular table. In your scale, 1 unit equals 2 feet. What is the perimeter of the table? _____

REVIEW

List the positive factors of these numbers. ◄13–18. MOC 056

13. 12 _____

14. 20 _____

15. 24 _____

16. 30 _____

17. 56 _____

18. 60 _____

Use your answers to questions 13–18. List the common factors of these number pairs. ◄19–21. MOC 065

19. 12, 20 _____

20. 20, 30 _____

21. 24, 60 _____

GLOSSARY TO GO

Today you will begin to create a math glossary to be used in school and at home. It will contain pictures and definitions of many math terms that you will encounter in math texts and tests. By writing your own definitions and keeping them in a notebook, you will be more likely to remember and understand these terms. You can use the glossary throughout the summer and as a resource during the next school year.

DIRECTIONS

- Put a marker or self-stick note on page 151 of this book.

- Each day, write definitions and draw pictures illustrating the new math terms. The vocabulary should be covered in your class time, so you should be familiar with most of the terms.

Numbers of Nim

Object: Remove the last counter from an array of 3 rows of counters.

MATERIALS

12 Counters

DIRECTIONS

1. If you are Player 2, turn to page 10. Arrange the 12 counters in the array.

2. Take turns removing any number of counters from any single row. Counters may not be removed from more than one row in a turn. As you remove counters, **explain** your thinking. **(You took 3 from the middle row, I think I will take 3 from the bottom row. That way, your next turn can't force me to give you a winning play.)**

3. If you remove the last counter, you win.

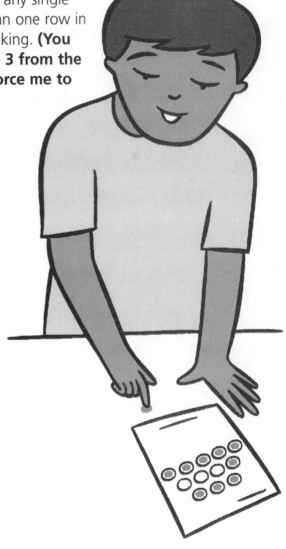

If I take the whole bottom row away, then you could take 2 from the top and leave me to choose whether to take 1 from the top or 1 from the middle. Whichever I chose, you could take the last counter. I think I will leave 2 on the bottom row.

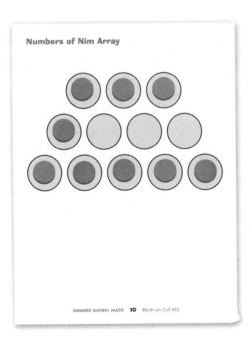

Numbers of Nim Array

Numbers of Nim Array

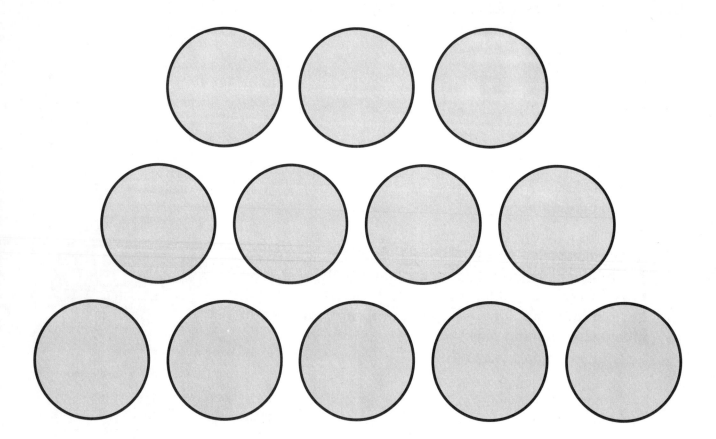

Name _____

Making a Double-Bar Graph

How do the numbers of gold medals won in the 2004 Summer Olympics compare to the numbers won in the 2002 Winter Olympics?

DIRECTIONS

- Work with a partner and use the blank graph on the next page.

- Decide on a scale and interval for your double-bar graph.

- Label and title your graph to represent the data.

- Make a double-bar graph of the data.

- Answer the questions to analyze the data.

2002 Winter Olympics

Country	Gold Medals
Australia	2
France	4
Germany	12
Italy	4
The Netherlands	3
People's Republic of China	2
Russian Federation	5
United States of America	10

Source: Olympics.org

2004 Summer Olympics

Country	Gold Medals
Australia	17
France	11
Germany	14
Italy	10
The Netherlands	4
People's Republic of China	32
Russian Federation	27
United States of America	35

ANALYZE THE DATA

1. Which country's athletes received the most gold medals in the winter Olympics, the summer Olympics, and the combined games?

   _____

2. What is the range of the number of gold medals earned by all of the countries during both Olympic Games? _____

3. Which country had the greatest difference between summer and winter medal counts?

   _____

Making a Double-Bar Graph

Title: _____

Name _____

NUMBER AND OPERATIONS

Shade each model to show $\frac{1}{4}$. ◀1–3. MOC 028

1.

2.

3.

Write $\frac{3}{4}$ two different ways. ◀4–5. MOC 044, 442

4. as a decimal: _____

5. as a percent: _____

PATTERNS AND ALGEBRA

Continue the pattern and answer the related questions. ◀6–9. MOC 132–135

6. $5\frac{3}{4}$, $5\frac{1}{2}$, $5\frac{1}{4}$, 5, _____, _____, _____

7. Which terms will be whole numbers if the pattern continues? _____

8. Which term will have a value of 3? _____

9. Describe the rule for the pattern.

_____

_____

_____

GEOMETRY AND MEASUREMENT

Use the diagram to answer the questions. ◀10–11. MOC 104, 346

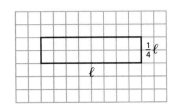

10. The width is $1\frac{1}{2}$ inches. What is the length? _____

11. What is the perimeter of this rectangle? _____

Draw the shape then name it. ◄12–13. MOC 363, 389

12. Draw a quadrilateral with only 2 lines of symmetry. Show the lines of symmetry.

13. Name your quadrilateral. _____

REVIEW

Solve mentally. ◄14–19. MOC 092, 120

14. $99 + 56 =$ _____

15. $201 - 155 =$ _____

16. $999 + 121 =$ _____

17. $10,001 - 500 =$ _____

18. $0.9 + 0.6 =$ _____

19. $1.1 - 0.5 =$ _____

Answer the questions. ◄20–26. MOC 026, 442

20. A dime is what percent of a dollar? _____

21. A quarter is what percent of a dollar? _____

22. A penny is what percent of a dollar? _____

23. A nickel is what percent of a dollar? _____

24. Three quarters is what percent of a dollar? _____

25. Ten dimes is what percent of a dollar? _____

26. Twelve dimes is what percent of a dollar? _____

GLOSSARY TO GO

Write definitions and draw pictures illustrating new math terms. The vocabulary should be covered in your class time, so you should be familiar with most of the terms.

Name _____

Comparing a Histogram with a Double-Bar Graph

How many countries received 20 or more gold medals during the 2002 Winter Olympics and 2004 Summer Olympics combined?

DIRECTIONS

- Work with a partner and use the blank graph on the next page.

- Decide on the scale and intervals for your histogram.

- Calculate how many countries fall into each interval.

- Title your graph.

- Make a histogram with the data.

- Answer the questions to analyze the data.

2002 Winter Olympics

Country	Gold Medals
Australia	2
France	4
Germany	12
Italy	4
The Netherlands	3
People's Republic of China	2
Russian Federation	5
United States of America	10

Source: Olympics.org

2004 Summer Olympics

Country	Gold Medals
Australia	17
France	11
Germany	14
Italy	10
The Netherlands	4
People's Republic of China	32
Russian Federation	27
United States of America	35

ANALYZE THE DATA

1. In which interval on the histogram is there the greatest frequency? Where is the least frequency?

_____

2. Compare your histogram with the double-bar graph of the same data on page 12. What kinds of questions are best answered by each kind of graph?

_____

_____

_____

3. What information is shown in the bar graph that is not shown in the histogram?

_____

Comparing a Histogram with a Double-Bar Graph

Title: _____

Name _____

NUMBER AND OPERATIONS

Shade each model to show $\frac{1}{3}$. ◄1–3. MOC 028

1.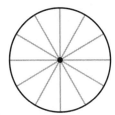

2.

3.

Complete the ratio table. ◄4. MOC 036

4.

1	$3\frac{1}{3}$	4	$33\frac{1}{3}$
3			

Write each number using repeating decimal notation. ◄5–6. MOC 023

5. $\frac{1}{3}$ _____

6. $33\frac{1}{3}\%$ _____

PATTERNS AND ALGEBRA

Continue the pattern and use it for the related problems. ◄7–9. MOC 104–107

7. 3, $3\frac{1}{3}$, $3\frac{2}{3}$, 4, $4\frac{1}{3}$, $4\frac{2}{3}$, _____, _____, _____

8. Which term will have a value of 6? _____

9. Describe the rule for the pattern.

_____

_____

_____

GEOMETRY AND MEASUREMENT

Draw the diagrams and answer the question. ◀ 10–11. MOC 351–352

10. Draw a triangle with no lines of symmetry.

11. Draw a diagram to help explain why you can't make a triangle with sides 3, 4, and 8 units long.

_____

_____

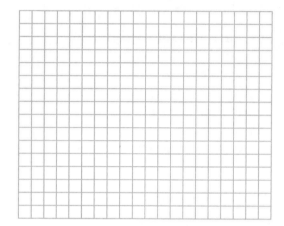

These triangles are similar. ◀ 12–13. MOC 351, 376

12. What is the measure of angle _A_? _____

13. What is the measure of angle _F_? _____

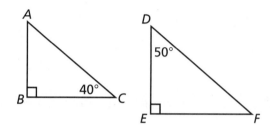

REVIEW

Use mental math. ◀ 14–21. MOC 145, 175

14. 10 × 4 = _____

15. 10 × 4.1 = _____

16. 100 × 4.1 = _____

17. 1,000 × 4.1 = _____

18. 40 ÷ 10 = _____

19. 4 ÷ 10 = _____

20. 4 ÷ 100 = _____

21. 4 ÷ 1,000 = _____

GLOSSARY TO GO

Write definitions and draw pictures illustrating new math terms. The vocabulary should be covered in your class time, so you should be familiar with most of the terms.

Fraction Sums

Object: Make 5 fractions whose sum is close to the target number, 3.

I still have 3 more turns, so I'll use the smaller fraction, $\frac{2}{3}$, to make my running sum $2\frac{1}{6}$.

MATERIALS

Two 1–6 number cubes, paper, pencil

DIRECTIONS

1. Make a recording sheet like the one shown. Fill in only the column heading and first column.

2. Roll the number cubes. Use the faceup digits to write a fraction on the recording sheet.

3. **Explain** why you chose the fraction. **(I rolled 2 and 3, so I can make either $\frac{2}{3}$ or $\frac{3}{2}$. Since my sum is already $1\frac{1}{2}$ and I have 3 more turns, I'll use $\frac{2}{3}$ to make a sum of $2\frac{1}{6}$.)**

4. Take turns for 5 rounds, adding the fractions on each turn.

5. If your final sum is closer to 3, either over under, you win.

Round	Fraction	Running Sum
1	$\frac{6}{4}$	$1\frac{1}{2}$
2	$\frac{2}{3}$	$2\frac{1}{6}$
3		
4		
5		

Name _____

Problem Solving: Rectangular Dimensions

DIRECTIONS

- Rewrite the problem in your own words.

- Show your work and complete the answer. Circle the strategies you used.

- Don't forget to use units.

PROBLEM 1

A rectangle has a perimeter of 60 centimeters. The width is $\frac{1}{2}$ of the length. What are the whole-number dimensions of the rectangle?

Width _____

Length _____

PROBLEM 2

A rectangle has a perimeter of 60 centimeters. The width is $\frac{1}{4}$ of the length. What are the dimensions of the rectangle?

Width _____

Length _____

ANALYZE YOUR WORK

1. Did your work on the first problem help you with the second problem? If so, how?

   _____

   _____

2. For Problem 2, what is the relationship between the perimeter and the dimensions? Write out the relationship using words and an equation.

   _____

   _____

   _____

NUMBER AND OPERATIONS

Shade each model to show $\frac{1}{5}$. ◄1–3. MOC 028

1. 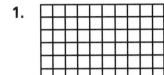   **2.** 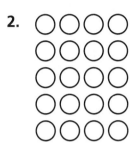   **3.**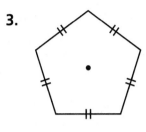

Write $\frac{1}{5}$ two different ways. ◄4–5. MOC 044, 442

4. as a decimal: _____

5. as a percent: _____

PATTERNS AND ALGEBRA

Continue the pattern and answer the related questions. ◄6–9. MOC 037–038, 107

6. $\frac{1}{10}$, $\frac{1}{5}$, $\frac{3}{10}$, $\frac{2}{5}$, $\frac{1}{2}$, _____, _____, _____

7. Repeat the pattern in Problem 6 using fractions with a common denominator.

_____, _____, _____, _____

_____, _____, _____, _____

8. Describe the rule for the pattern.

_____

_____

_____

9. Repeat the pattern in Problem 6 using decimals.

_____, _____, _____, _____,

_____, _____, _____, _____

GEOMETRY AND MEASUREMENT

Use the diagram to answer the questions. ◄10. MOC 346, 11. MOC 377, 12. MOC 535

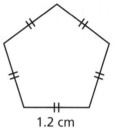

1.2 cm

10. One side of this regular pentagon is
1.2 centimeters. What is the perimeter? _____

11. If this is a scale drawing for a garden room and the scale is
1 centimeter = 5 meters, what is the perimeter of the room? _____

12. How many centimeters is that? _____

REVIEW

Use mental math. ◄13–27. MOC 152, 161

13. $5 \times 7 =$ _____

14. $6 \times 7 =$ _____

15. $7 \times 7 =$ _____

16. $8 \times 7 =$ _____

17. $9 \times 7 =$ _____

18. $10 \times 5 =$ _____

19. $10 \times 7 =$ _____

20. $10 \times 9 =$ _____

21. $10 \times 10 =$ _____

22. $10 \times 11 =$ _____

23. $\frac{1}{2}$ of 16 = _____

24. $\frac{1}{2}$ of 24 = _____

25. $\frac{1}{2}$ of 50 = _____

26. $\frac{1}{2}$ of 66 = _____

27. $\frac{1}{2}$ of 98 = _____

GLOSSARY TO GO

Write definitions and draw pictures illustrating new math terms. The vocabulary
should be covered in your class time, so you should be familiar with most of
the terms.

Name _____

Problem Solving: Spending Money

DIRECTIONS

- Rewrite the problem in your own words.

- Show your work. Circle the strategies you used.

PROBLEM 1

José put $\frac{1}{2}$ of his money in the bank. He spent $\frac{1}{3}$ of his remaining money on books. He has $18 left. How much money did he start with? _____

PROBLEM 2

Maria put $\frac{1}{5}$ of her money in the bank. She spent $\frac{1}{2}$ of her remaining money on books. She has $10 left. How much money did she start with? _____

ANALYZE YOUR WORK

1. Did your work on the first problem help you with the second problem? If so, how?

   _____

   _____

2. If you didn't make a model or diagram while solving Problem 2, make one now and use it to show what part of the whole is taken away at each step, and how much money Maria started with.

Name _____

NUMBER AND OPERATIONS

Shade each model to show $\frac{1}{6}$. ◄1–3. MOC 028

1.

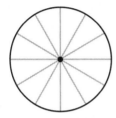

2.

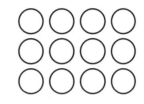

3.

Write $\frac{1}{6}$ two different ways. ◄4–5. MOC 023, 044, 442

4. as a decimal: _____

5. as a percent: _____

Answer the question. ◄6. MOC 023

6. Describe the difference between a repeating decimal and a terminating decimal.

_____

_____

_____

PATTERNS AND ALGEBRA

Continue the pattern and answer the related questions. ◄7–9. MOC 106–107, 442

7. $16\frac{2}{3}\%$, $33\frac{1}{3}\%$, 50%, $66\frac{2}{3}\%$, _____, _____, _____

8. Repeat the pattern in Question 7 using fractions. _____, _____, _____,

_____, _____, _____, _____

9. Describe the rule for the pattern.

_____

_____

Solve the problem. ◄10. MOC 161

10. Which is less money, $\frac{1}{6}$ of $100 or $\frac{1}{3}$ of $50?

_____

GEOMETRY AND MEASUREMENT

Draw the shape then answer the related question. ◀11–12. MOC 342, 387, 389

11. Complete the diagram of a hexagon that has only 2 lines of symmetry. Include the lines of symmetry.

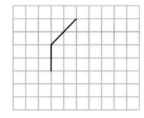

12. How many degrees will it turn before it matches itself?

_____

REVIEW

Complete the table. ◀13–17. MOC 044, 442

	Fraction	Decimal	Percent
13.	$\frac{1}{2}$		
14.	$\frac{1}{4}$		
15.	$\frac{1}{3}$		
16.	$\frac{1}{5}$		
17.	$\frac{1}{6}$		

Fill in the blanks. ◀18–24. MOC 161

18. $\frac{1}{4}$ of 8 = _____

19. $\frac{2}{4}$ of 8 = _____

20. $\frac{3}{4}$ of 8 = _____

21. $\frac{1}{5}$ of 8 = _____

22. $\frac{2}{5}$ of 8 = _____

23. $\frac{3}{5}$ of 8 = _____

24. $\frac{4}{5}$ of 8 = _____

GLOSSARY TO GO

Review the definitions and illustrations you added to your Glossary this week. Make additions or corrections if you need to.

Name _____

Problem Solving: Shaded Rectangles

DIRECTIONS

- Rewrite the problem in your own words.
- Show your work and complete the answer.
- Circle the strategies you used.

Figure 1

PROBLEM 1

A. What fraction of each of these figures is shaded? _____

Figure 2

B. What fractions of Figures 4 and 5 will be shaded? _____

C. If the pattern continues, what fraction of Figure 10 will be shaded? _____

Figure 3

D. What is a general rule for how many squares will be shaded in any figure? _____

PROBLEM 2

Figure 1

A. What fraction of each of these figures is shaded? _____

B. What fractions of Figures 4 and 5 will be shaded? _____

Figure 2

C. If the pattern continues, what fraction of Figure 10 will be shaded? _____

D. What is a general rule for how many squares will be shaded in any figure? _____

Figure 3

ANALYZE YOUR WORK

Compare the pattern you found for Problem 1 with the one you found for Problem 2. How are they similar? How are they different?

_____

_____

_____

NEWSLETTER

Summer Success: Math

This week, the students have reviewed many math skills.

Much of this week's work focused on fractions, decimals, and percents and how to write any given number in any of these 3 forms. You can help your child every time one of these number types comes up in conversation, while you watch the evening news, or while you're out shopping together. Talk about the number, then ask your child to use its other forms in context. For example,

- I see that Perry's Pants is having a 25%-off sale! What does that mean? (You pay $\frac{1}{4}$ less.) What fraction of the original price is the new price? ($\frac{3}{4}$) What percent is that? (75%)

- The weather reporter says there's a 75% chance of rain tomorrow. What does that mean? (It's more likely than not that it will rain.) What's the chance that it won't rain tomorrow? (25%) What fraction is that? ($\frac{1}{4}$)

 Thank you for talking with your child about math. Enjoy your time together.

Play Concentration

- Cut out the cards or copy them on index cards.
- Shuffle them and place them facedown in a 3 × 4 array.
- Take turns turning over 2 cards.
- If the numbers on your cards are equal, keep them and take another turn. Otherwise, turn them back over and let your partner take a turn.

$\frac{1}{3}$	$0.\overline{3}$	$\frac{1}{2}$	50%
$\frac{1}{4}$	0.25	$\frac{1}{5}$	20%
$\frac{1}{6}$	$0.1\overline{6}$	$\frac{2}{3}$	$66\frac{2}{3}\%$

 Enjoy these activities with your child. Remember that using math in the real world helps your child understand that math is important in school.

Name _____

NUMBER AND OPERATIONS

Shade each model to show $\frac{2}{3}$. ◄1–2. MOC 028

1.

2. ○○○○○○○○○
○○○○○○○○○

Place point _F_ about $\frac{2}{3}$ of the way from _E_ to _G_. ◄3. MOC 028

3. ●————————————————●
E   G

Write $\frac{2}{3}$ in two different ways. ◄4–5. MOC 044, 442

4. as a decimal: _____

5. as a percent: _____

Solve. ◄6–8. MOC 135

6. $1\frac{2}{3} - \frac{1}{2} =$ _____

7. $2 - \frac{2}{3}$ _____

8. Is $\frac{2}{3}$ closer to $\frac{1}{2}$ or to 1? _____

PATTERNS AND ALGEBRA

Continue the patterns and give a rule. ◄9–11. MOC 106

9. $33\frac{1}{3}\%$, $66\frac{2}{3}\%$, 100%, $133\frac{1}{3}\%$, _____, _____, _____

10. Repeat the pattern in Problem 9 using fractions. _____, _____, _____,

_____, _____, _____, _____

11. Describe how to find each term in the pattern in Problem 9.

_____

_____

GEOMETRY AND MEASUREMENT

Draw the shape and then answer the related questions. ◄ 12–15. MOC 342–343, 351, 354

12. Draw a regular triangle with sides 3 units long.
    Name your shape.

    _____

13. What is the perimeter of this triangle? _____

14. What is the measure of each of its interior angles? _____

15. What is the measure of each of its exterior angles? _____

REVIEW

Solve these problems. ◄ 16–20. MOC 102, 131, 158, 184

16. In a 3-day bike race, the bikers rode 50.5 kilometers on the first day, 40.5 kilometers on the second day, and 67.7 kilometers on the third day. How far did they ride in the 3 days?

    _____

17. One bike weighs 12.6 kilograms and another bike weighs 9.8 kilograms. How much heavier is the first bike?

    _____

18. One biker rode at an average speed of 10.1 kilometers per hour. How far did he ride in 5 hours?

    _____

19. Another biker rode at an average speed of 15.1 kilometers per hour. If she rode 120.8 kilometers, how many hours did she ride?

    _____

20. How much faster did the biker in Problem 19 ride than the biker in Problem 18?

    _____

GLOSSARY TO GO

Write definitions and draw pictures illustrating new math terms. The vocabulary should be covered in your class time, so you should be familiar with most of the terms.

Fraction Time

Object: Add fractions of an hour to get a sum close to 3 hours.

MATERIALS

Two 1–6 number cubes, pencils

DIRECTIONS

1. If you are Player 2, turn to page 34. You will both use the same recording sheet.

2. Take turns rolling the number cubes. Use the digits to make a fraction less than or equal to one.

3. Record the fraction and figure out how many minutes are in that fractional part of one hour.

4. Decide whether you will take those minutes or the minutes that are left in an hour as your score for the round. Your partner gets the minutes you don't take. **Explain** your thinking. **(I already have more than 60 minutes and there are 3 more rounds. I'll take $\frac{1}{3}$ of an hour and give you $\frac{2}{3}$ of an hour.)**

5. After 6 rounds, add your minutes. Rewrite them as hours and minutes. If your total is closer to 3 hours, you win.

> I'll take $\frac{1}{3}$ of an hour and give you $\frac{2}{3}$ of an hour because I don't want to get close to 3 hours too soon.

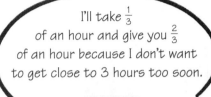

Round		Player 1	Player 2
1	Fraction	$\frac{4}{5}$	$\frac{1}{5}$
	Minutes	$\frac{4}{5} \times 60 = 48$	12
2	Fraction	$\frac{1}{4}$	$\frac{3}{4}$
	Minutes	15	$\frac{3}{4} \times 60 = 45$
3	Fraction	$\frac{1}{3}$	$\frac{2}{3}$
	Minutes		

Fraction Time Recording Sheet

Round		Player 1	Player 2
1	Fraction		
	Minutes		
2	Fraction		
	Minutes		
3	Fraction		
	Minutes		
4	Fraction		
	Minutes		
5	Fraction		
	Minutes		
6	Fraction		
	Minutes		
Total minutes			
Hours : minutes			

Round		Player 1	Player 2
1	Fraction		
	Minutes		
2	Fraction		
	Minutes		
3	Fraction		
	Minutes		
4	Fraction		
	Minutes		
5	Fraction		
	Minutes		
6	Fraction		
	Minutes		
Total minutes			
Hours : minutes			

▢ = player who rolled the cubes

Name _____

Making a Stem-and-Leaf Plot

How do the top speeds of some of the world's fastest land animals compare to a human's top speed?

DIRECTIONS

- Work with a partner.

- Decide how you will divide the numbers into stems and leaves, and what the stems will be for your stem-and-leaf plot.

- Title your plot and plot the *Top Speed* data on the next page.

- Write a key that explains how to read the stems and leaves.

- Answer the questions to analyze the data.

Some Fast Land Animals

Adult Animal	Top Speed (mph)	Average Height (inches)
Cheetah	70	36
Coyote	43	20
Elk	45	65
Greyhound	39	29
Human	28	66
Hyena	40	34
Lion	50	40
Ostrich	45	92
Wildebeest	50	50

Source: homeworkspot.com

ANALYZE THE DATA

1. Where did most of the speeds fall on the stem-and-leaf plot? _____

2. Use your plot to find the median for the data set. Compare the median to the slowest time.

   Median: _____

   The median time is _____

3. How does the mean compare to the median?

   _____

Making a Stem-and-Leaf Plot

Title: _____

Stem	Leaves

Key: _____

Name _____

NUMBER AND OPERATIONS

Write $\frac{5}{6}$ in 2 different ways. ◀1–2. MOC 044, 442

1. as a decimal: _____

2. as a percent: _____

Name each lettered point on the number line with a fraction and a decimal. ◀3–5. MOC 023

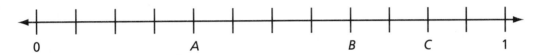

0   A   B   C   1

3. A _____

4. B _____

5. C _____

Solve. ◀6–7. MOC 107, 135

6. $1\frac{5}{6} - \frac{1}{2} =$ _____

7. $1\frac{5}{6} + 1\frac{1}{2} =$ _____

PATTERNS AND ALGEBRA

Use the pattern in problem 8 for problems 9 and 10. ◀8–10. MOC 132–135

8. $5\frac{1}{3}$, $5\frac{1}{6}$, 5, $4\frac{5}{6}$, $4\frac{2}{3}$, _____, _____, _____

9. What will be the value of term 12? _____

10. Describe how to find a term in the pattern.

_____

_____

GEOMETRY AND MEASUREMENT

Draw the shape and then answer the related questions. ◀ 11–14. MOC 161, 346

11. Draw a regular polygon with 6 sides, each 2 units long. Name your shape.

_____

12. What is the perimeter of this polygon? _____

13. What is the perimeter of a similar figure with sides $\frac{5}{6}$ as long?

_____

14. What is the length of each side of this similar polygon? _____

REVIEW

Find each sum or difference. ◀ 15–22. MOC 104–107, 132–135

15. $\frac{2}{3} + \frac{1}{6} =$ _____

16. $\frac{2}{3} - \frac{1}{6} =$ _____

17. $4 + \frac{2}{3} =$ _____

18. $4 - \frac{2}{3} =$ _____

19. $4\frac{1}{3} + \frac{1}{6} =$ _____

20. $4\frac{1}{3} - \frac{1}{6} =$ _____

21. $4\frac{1}{2} + \frac{5}{6} =$ _____

22. $4\frac{1}{2} - \frac{5}{6} =$ _____

GLOSSARY TO GO

Write definitions and draw pictures illustrating new math terms. The vocabulary should be covered in your class time, so you should be familiar with most of the terms.

Comparing a Scatter Plot to a Stem-and-Leaf Plot

Is the height of an animal related to its top speed?

DIRECTIONS

- Work with a partner and use the blank graph on the next page.
- Decide on the scale and intervals for your scatter plot.
- Title your graph.
- Graph the data.
- Answer the questions to analyze the data.

Some Fast Land Animals

Adult Animal	Average Height (inches)	Top Speed (mph)
Cheetah	36	70
Coyote	20	43
Elk	65	45
Greyhound	29	39
Human	66	28
Hyena	34	40
Lion	40	50
Ostrich	92	45
Wildebeest	50	50

Source: homeworkspot.com

ANALYZE THE DATA

1. For this list of animals, do you see any relationship between speed and height?

   _____

   _____

2. Do you think that adding some slower animals, like turtles and sloths, to the list would change your thinking about the relationship of height to speed?

   _____

   _____

3. Is it easier to find the median speed from a scatter plot or a stem-and-leaf plot?

   _____

4. What do you look at in each plot to get a sense of the speed at which fast animals tend to run?

   _____

   _____

Comparing a Scatter Plot to a Stem-and-Leaf Plot

Title: _____

_____

NUMBER AND OPERATIONS

Write the fractions in order from least to greatest. ◄1. MOC 036–041

1. $\frac{5}{8}, \frac{1}{2}, \frac{7}{8}, \frac{1}{4}, \frac{1}{8}, \frac{3}{4}, \frac{3}{8}$ _____

Write $\frac{7}{8}$ in 2 different ways. ◄2–3. MOC 044, 442

2. as a decimal: _____

3. as a percent: _____

Write and solve an equation. ◄4–5. MOC 134–135

4. How much less is $\frac{5}{8}$ of a quart than $\frac{7}{8}$ of a quart?

_____

5. How much more is $\frac{7}{8}$ of a pound than $\frac{1}{2}$ of a pound?

_____

PATTERNS AND ALGEBRA

Use the pattern in problem 6 to solve problems 7 and 8. ◄6–8. MOC 104–107

6. $1\frac{1}{8}, 1\frac{1}{2}, 1\frac{7}{8}, 2\frac{1}{4},$ _____, _____, _____

7. What will be the value of term 10? _____

8. Describe how to find the next term in the pattern.

_____

GEOMETRY AND MEASUREMENT

Draw the shape and then answer the related question. ◄9–10. MOC 342

9. Draw a concave octagon that is different from the one on today's Geometry Recording Pad. Try to give it at least 2 interior angles greater than 180°.

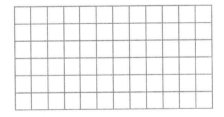

10. What is the sum of the interior angle measures of this octagon? _____

REVIEW

Write the numerators to complete each statement. ◄11–18. MOC 036

11. $\frac{1}{2}$ is equivalent to $\frac{\boxed{}}{4}$, $\frac{\boxed{}}{6}$, $\frac{\boxed{}}{8}$.

12. $\frac{1}{3}$ is equivalent to $\frac{\boxed{}}{6}$, $\frac{\boxed{}}{9}$, $\frac{\boxed{}}{12}$.

13. $\frac{1}{4}$ is equivalent to $\frac{\boxed{}}{8}$, $\frac{\boxed{}}{12}$, $\frac{\boxed{}}{16}$.

14. $\frac{1}{5}$ is equivalent to $\frac{\boxed{}}{10}$, $\frac{\boxed{}}{15}$, $\frac{\boxed{}}{20}$.

15. $\frac{1}{6}$ is equivalent to $\frac{\boxed{}}{12}$, $\frac{\boxed{}}{18}$, $\frac{\boxed{}}{24}$.

16. $\frac{2}{3}$ is equivalent to $\frac{\boxed{}}{6}$, $\frac{\boxed{}}{9}$, $\frac{\boxed{}}{12}$.

17. $\frac{5}{6}$ is equivalent to $\frac{\boxed{}}{12}$, $\frac{\boxed{}}{18}$, $\frac{\boxed{}}{24}$.

18. $\frac{7}{8}$ is equivalent to $\frac{\boxed{}}{16}$, $\frac{\boxed{}}{24}$, $\frac{\boxed{}}{32}$.

Compare. Write <, >, or =. ◄19–26. MOC 039–040

19. $\frac{1}{6}$ ◯ $\frac{1}{3}$ **20.** $\frac{1}{2}$ ◯ $\frac{1}{6}$

21. $\frac{1}{3}$ ◯ $\frac{1}{4}$ **22.** $\frac{1}{5}$ ◯ $\frac{1}{4}$

23. $\frac{1}{6}$ ◯ $\frac{1}{8}$ **24.** $\frac{2}{3}$ ◯ $\frac{5}{6}$

25. $\frac{4}{6}$ ◯ $\frac{2}{3}$ **26.** $\frac{5}{6}$ ◯ $\frac{7}{8}$

GLOSSARY TO GO

Write definitions and draw pictures illustrating new math terms. The vocabulary should be covered in your class time, so you should be familiar with most of the terms.

Percent Sense

Object: Cover four percents in a row by making equivalent fractions.

MATERIALS

Percent Sense Game Board; counters: 10 each of 2 colors; 2 paper clips

DIRECTIONS

1. Choose the counter color to mark your plays.

2. If you are Player 1, place the paper clips on 1 or 2 numbers at the bottom of the Game Board. Form a fraction with your numbers. Place one of your counters on the Game Board on the percent equivalent to this fraction.

3. If you are Player 2, move just one of the paper clips to another number. Form a new fraction and place a counter on any free space on the Game Board that contains the equivalent percent.

4. Take turns moving a clip, making a fraction, and finding its equivalent percent. **Explain** your move. **(I can use $\frac{10}{10} = 100\%$ to get 2 in a row in the fifth column.)**

5. If you are first to get 4 counters in a row vertically, horizontally, or diagonally, you win.

50%	$66\frac{2}{3}\%$	$83\frac{1}{3}\%$	25%	$37\frac{1}{2}\%$	$33\frac{1}{3}\%$
$12\frac{1}{2}\%$	80%	30%	$62\frac{1}{2}\%$	100%	60%
40%	20%	$33\frac{1}{3}\%$	75%	$16\frac{2}{3}\%$	10%
60%	10%	$37\frac{1}{2}\%$	$66\frac{2}{3}\%$	40%	100%
$66\frac{2}{3}\%$	100%	20%	$83\frac{1}{3}\%$	$62\frac{1}{2}\%$	50%
25%	$16\frac{2}{3}\%$	50%	$12\frac{1}{2}\%$	75%	30%

1   2   3   4   5   6   8   10

If I leave the clip on 10 and move the other clip to 10, I can make 1, which is 100%. I can use that to block you in the second row.

Name _____

Problem Solving: Combining Money

DIRECTIONS

- Rewrite the problem in your own words.

- Show your work and complete the answer. Circle the strategies you used.

PROBLEM 1

Together, Valerie and Penelope have $55. Valerie has $\frac{5}{6}$ as much money as Penelope has.

How much does Valerie have? _____

How much does Penelope have? _____

PROBLEM 2

Together, Lyman and Jesse have $60. Lyman has $\frac{7}{8}$ as much money as Jesse.

How much does Lyman have? _____ How much money does Jesse have? _____

ANALYZE YOUR WORK

1. Did your work on the first problem help you with the second problem? If so, how?

_____

2. If you didn't use the *Write an Equation* strategy, write and solve an equation for Problem 2 now.

_____

Name _____

NUMBER AND OPERATIONS

Compare. Use <, >, or =. ◂1–3. MOC 040, 044, 442

1. $\frac{9}{10}$ ◯ 90%

2. $\frac{9}{10}$ ◯ 0.89

3. $\frac{9}{10}$ ◯ $\frac{16}{20}$

Write $\frac{9}{10}$ in 2 different ways. ◂4–5. MOC 044, 442

4. as a decimal: _____

5. as a percent: _____

Use mental math to find each answer. ◂6–8. MOC 143–148

6. $\frac{9}{10}$ of $2.00 = _____

7. $\frac{9}{10}$ of $25.00 = _____

8. 90% of $7.00 = _____

PATTERNS AND ALGEBRA

Use a pattern to complete the table. Then describe the rule. ◂9–14. MOC 161, 187–188

	1	$\frac{9}{10}$
	2	$\frac{18}{10}$
9.		$\frac{27}{10}$
10.	5	
11.	10	
12.		$\frac{108}{10}$
13.		$\frac{279}{10}$

14. Describe the rule used to complete the table.

_____

_____

GEOMETRY AND MEASUREMENT

Draw the shape and then answer the related question. ◀15. MOC 363, 376, 16. MOC 365, 17. MOC 366

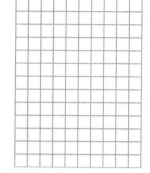

15. Draw 2 similar rectangles. Make one rectangle twice as long and twice as wide as the other. Label the sides appropriately.

16. How do the perimeters of these rectangles compare?

_____

_____

17. How do their areas compare?

_____

REVIEW

Complete the table. ◀18–22. MOC 031, 044, 442

	Fraction	Word Form	Decimal	Percent
18.	$\frac{1}{3}$			
19.	$\frac{1}{6}$			
20.	$\frac{2}{3}$			
21.	$\frac{5}{6}$			
22.	$\frac{7}{8}$			

Each lettered section is what percent of the large square? ◀23–26. MOC 026, 028, 044, 442

23. A _____

24. B _____

25. C _____

26. D _____

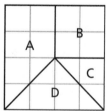

GLOSSARY TO GO

Write definitions and draw pictures illustrating new math terms. The vocabulary should be covered in your class time, so you should be familiar with most of the terms.

Problem Solving: Similar Rectangles

DIRECTIONS

- Rewrite the problem in your own words; draw a diagram on page 48 if it helps.

- Show your work and complete the answer. Circle the strategies you used.

- Don't forget to use units.

POSSIBLE STRATEGIES

- Guess, Check, and Revise

- Make a Table or an Organized List

- Write an Equation

- Make a Model or a Diagram

- Look for Patterns

- Other _____

PROBLEM 1

There are 2 similar rectangles. Rectangle *A* has a width of 6 centimeters and a length of 9 centimeters. Rectangle *B* has a perimeter of 40 centimeters. What are the dimensions of Rectangle *B*?

width: _____

length: _____

PROBLEM 2

There are 2 similar rectangles. Rectangle *A* has a width of 8 centimeters and a length of 10 centimeters. Rectangle *B* has a perimeter of 90 centimeters. What are the dimensions of Rectangle *B*?

width: _____

length: _____

ANALYZE YOUR WORK

1. Did your work on the first problem help you with the second problem? If so, how?

   _____

2. If you didn't use the *Write an Equation* strategy for Problem 2, write one now for Rectangle *B*.

Problem Solving: Similar Rectangles

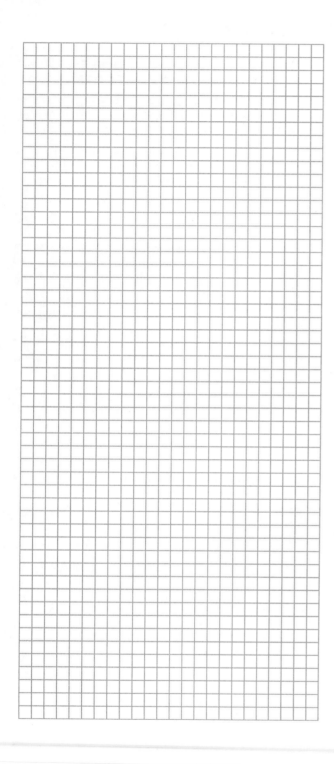

Name _____

NUMBER AND OPERATIONS

Name each lettered point on the number line as a fraction and as a decimal. ◂1–3. MOC 023, 044

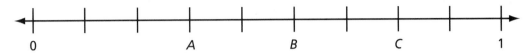

1. A _____

2. B _____

3. C _____

Write $\frac{8}{9}$ in 2 different ways. ◂4–5. MOC 044, 442

4. as a decimal: _____

5. as a percent: _____

Use mental math to find each answer. ◂6–8. MOC 143–148

6. $\frac{8}{9}$ of $27 = _____

7. $\frac{8}{9}$ of $36 = _____

8. $\frac{8}{9}$ of $63 = _____

Solve the problem. ◂9–10. MOC 161

9. Darnell had $54.00. He earned $\frac{8}{9}$ of that amount mowing lawns. How much money did Darnell earn mowing lawns?

    _____

10. Alex can ride a mile in 3 minutes. He usually rides an $\frac{8}{9}$ mile route near his home. How long does it take him to ride the route near his home?

    _____

PATTERNS AND ALGEBRA

Continue and describe the pattern. ◂11–12. MOC 132

11. $6\frac{1}{9}$, $5\frac{2}{9}$, $4\frac{1}{3}$, $3\frac{4}{9}$, _____, _____, _____

12. Describe how to find the next term in the pattern.

    _____

    _____

GEOMETRY AND MEASUREMENT

Answer the related questions. ◀13–15. MOC 346, 377

13. What is the perimeter of a nine-sided regular polygon with a side 9 centimeters long?

_____

14. A similar polygon has a perimeter that is $\frac{8}{9}$ of the one in Problem 13. What is its perimeter?

_____

15. What is the length of each side of the polygon in Problem 14? _____

REVIEW

Find the products and quotients. ◀16–23. MOC 145, 175

16. $10 \times 3.12 =$ _____

17. $100 \times 3.12 =$ _____

18. $1,000 \times 3.12 =$ _____

19. $10,000 \times 3.12 =$ _____

20. $3.12 \div 10 =$ _____

21. $3.12 \div 100 =$ _____

22. $3.12 \div 1,000 =$ _____

23. $3.12 \div 10,000 =$ _____

GLOSSARY TO GO

Review the definitions and illustrations you added to your Glossary this week.
Make additions or corrections if you need to.

PROBLEM SOLVING

Problem Solving: Similar Polygons

DIRECTIONS

- Rewrite the problem in your own words. Draw a diagram on the back of this page if it helps.

- Show your work. Circle the strategies you used.

- Don't forget to use units.

POSSIBLE STRATEGIES

- Guess, Check, and Revise

- Write an Equation

- Make a Model or a Diagram

- Other _____

PROBLEM 1

A regular pentagon, A, has sides 16 centimeters long. A similar pentagon, B, has sides that are $\frac{7}{8}$ as long as A's. What is the perimeter of Pentagon B?

_____

_____

_____

PROBLEM 2

A regular octagon, A, has sides 27 centimeters long. A similar octagon, B, has sides that are $\frac{8}{9}$ as long as A's. What is the perimeter of Octagon B?

_____

_____

_____

ANALYZE YOUR WORK

1. Did your work on the first problem help you with the second problem? If so, how?

_____

_____

2. If you didn't use the *Write an Equation* strategy for Problem 2, write and solve one now.

_____

Summer Success: Math

This week, we continued to work with fractions and we also studied characteristics of geometric figures.

You can help your child feel more comfortable with geometry and its very specific vocabulary by asking him or her to describe everyday shapes using mathematical terms. For example,

- Can you help me describe the living room to the wallpaper salesperson?

- Let's use geometric terms to name all of the highway signs we see. (For example, caution signs are triangles, stop signs are octagons, speed limit signs are rectangles.)

On the back of this page is a list of shapes. Ask your child to show you some items in or near your home that incorporate these shapes.

 Enjoy your time with your child, and thank you for helping to strengthen your child's comfort with important math concepts.

Search for shapes in and near your home.

Shape	Object
an octagon	
a concave polygon	
a regular polygon	
2 similar shapes	
a set of supplementary angles	

Show your child that you're proud of his or her progress. Remember that using math in the real world will help your child understand that math is important in school.

Name _____

NUMBER AND OPERATIONS

Answer each question. ◄1–2. MOC 046

1. What is the opposite of 1? _____

2. On the number line, is −1 to the left or to the right of zero? _____

Use the number line to find the sum. ◄3–5. MOC 108

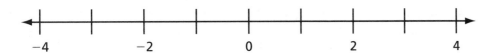

3. What is 1 + (−1)? _____

4. What is 2 + (−4)? _____

5. 1 + (−1) + (−1) = _____

PATTERNS AND ALGEBRA

Write an addition equation for the diagram. ◄6–7. MOC 108

6.
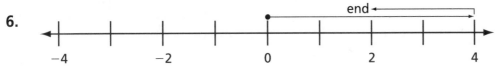

_____

7.
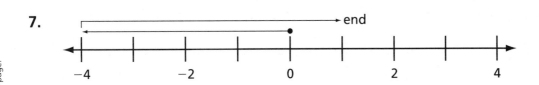

_____

Write the missing numbers. ◄8–11. MOC 108

8. −1 + _____ = 2

9. −1 + _____ = −2

10. −1 + _____ = 0

11. −1 + _____ = −3

GEOMETRY AND MEASUREMENT

Draw a coordinate grid and then answer the related question. ◀ 12–14. MOC 318–320

12. Draw a coordinate grid. Label the *x*- and *y*-axes from −6 through 6.

13. Plot and label point (−2, 4).

14. Plot and label point (4, −2).

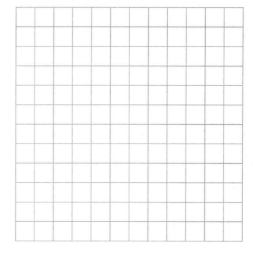

REVIEW

Find each product or quotient. ◀ 15–25. MOC 144, 175

15. 15 × 10 = _____

16. 15 × 1 = _____

17. 15 × 0.1 = _____

18. 15 × 0.01 = _____

19. 15 × 0.001 = _____

20. 15 ÷ 1,000 = _____

21. 15 ÷ 100 = _____

22. 15 ÷ 10 = _____

23. 15 ÷ 1 = _____

24. 15 ÷ 0.1 = _____

25. What mental-math patterns do you use when you multiply and divide by tens?

_____

_____

_____

GLOSSARY TO GO

Write definitions and draw pictures illustrating new math terms. The vocabulary should be covered in your class time, so you should be familiar with most of the terms.

Pick An Integer

Object: Mark 3 coordinate pairs in a row.

MATERIALS

Integer Cards (26 cards), 2 different-colored pencils, paper bag

DIRECTIONS

1. If you are Player 2, turn to page 58. You will both play each game on the same grid. Choose the color to mark your plays. Place the Integer Cards in the paper bag and shake well.

2. Take turns. Draw 2 Integer Cards from the bag and use them as coordinates of a point on the Game Board. **Explain** your choice. **(I drew 5 and –3. Both (5, –3) and (–3, 5) are open, but I can block you if I choose (–3, 5).)**

3. Mark the selected point and return the Integer Cards to the bag. Shake well.

4. Once a point is marked, it may not be marked again. If both possible points are marked, you lose your turn.

5. If you are first to mark 3 points in a row, vertically, horizontally, or diagonally, you win.

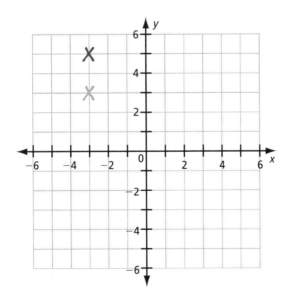

Pick An Integer Game Board

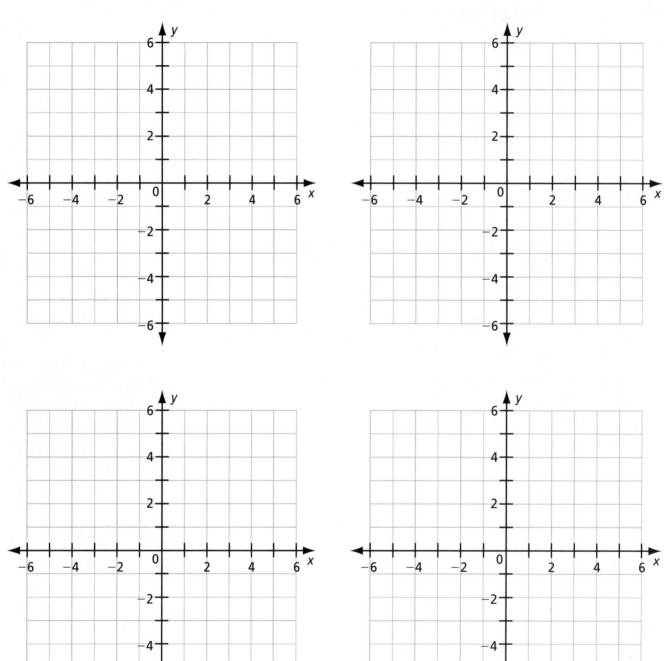

Name _____

Making a Circle Graph

Is population a good way to predict the number of Internet users in a country?

MATERIALS

Colored pencils

DIRECTIONS

- Study the table. It shows the 10 countries with the highest world-wide Internet use, each country's percent of the users in those 10 countries, and each country's percent of the population of those 10 countries. For example, 3.5% of the Internet users in the top 10 countries live in Brazil, while 7% of the population of those countries lives in Brazil.

- Work with a partner to graph the data in column 2 on the next page. The U.S. is graphed for you.

- Write a key that explains how to read your graph.

- Answer the questions to analyze the data.

2005 Top 10 Internet-Use Countries

Country	Percent of Total Population of Top 10	Percent of Top 10 Internet Users
Brazil	7	3.5
China	35	16
France	2	4
Germany	3	8
India	34	6.5
Italy	2	5
Japan	4	13
South Korea	1	5
United Kingdom	2	6
United States	10	33
Total	100%	100%

Adapted from: Internetworldstats.com

ANALYZE THE DATA

Study the circle graph and tell 3 points the display emphasizes.

_____

_____

_____

_____

Making a Circle Graph

Title: _____

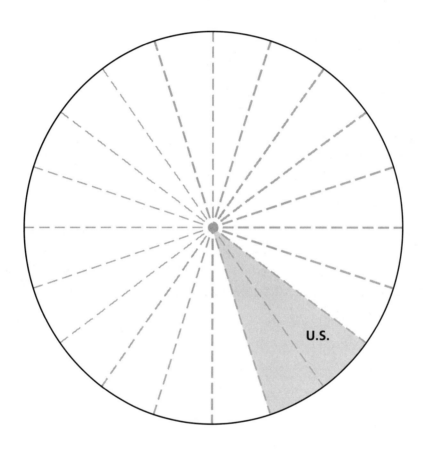

Name _____

NUMBER AND OPERATIONS

Answer each question. ◀1. MOC 046, 2–3. MOC 318

1. What is the opposite of 2? _____

2. On the *x*-axis, is −2 to the left or the right of 0? _____

3. On the *y*-axis, is −2 above or below 0? _____

Use the number line to show how to solve the equation. ◀4–5. MOC 108

4. 2 + (−2) = _____

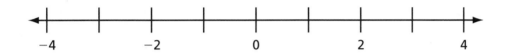

5. 2 − (−2) means *2 is how much more than −2*? _____

Compare. Write < or >. ◀6–8. MOC 48

6. −2 ◯ −1

7. 0 ◯ −2

8. −2 ◯ −4

PATTERNS AND ALGEBRA

Continue the pattern and write the rules. ◀9–11. MOC 204

9. 10, 8, 6, 4, _____, _____, _____

10. Write a subtraction rule that tells how to get from a term to the next term.

_____

11. Write a rule for finding term *n*. _____

GEOMETRY AND MEASUREMENT

Draw a coordinate grid and then answer the related question. ◀12. MOC 318–320, 13. MOC 363

12. Draw a coordinate grid. Label the *x*- and *y*-axes. Label and connect these points in order: (1, 0), (0, −2), (3, −2), (4, 0), and (1, 0).

13. Name the figure you drew in Problem 12.

_____

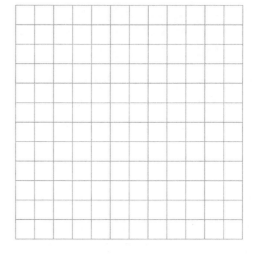

REVIEW

Write each fraction in 2 ways. ◀14–23. MOC 044, 442

	Fraction	Decimal	Percent
14.	$\frac{1}{2}$		
15.	$\frac{1}{4}$		
16.	$\frac{1}{3}$		
17.	$\frac{1}{5}$		
18.	$\frac{1}{6}$		
19.	$\frac{2}{3}$		
20.	$\frac{5}{6}$		
21.	$\frac{7}{8}$		
22.	$\frac{9}{10}$		
23.	$\frac{8}{9}$		

GLOSSARY TO GO

Write definitions and draw pictures illustrating new math terms. The vocabulary should be covered in your class time, so you should be familiar with most of the terms.

Name _____

Comparing a Circle Graph and a Histogram

Is population a good way to predict the number of internet users in a country?

MATERIALS

Colored pencils

DIRECTIONS

- Work with a partner.

- Decide on the scale and intervals for the histogram on the next page.

- Graph the data from column 3 on both the circle graph and the histogram. Italy is done for you.

- Answer the questions to analyze the data.

2005 Top 10 Internet-Use Countries

Country	Percent of Total Population of Top 10	Percent of Top 10 Internet Users
Brazil	7	3.5
China	35	16
France	2	4
Germany	3	8
India	34	6.5
Italy	2	5
Japan	4	13
South Korea	1	5
United Kingdom	2	6
United States	10	33
Total	100%	100%

Adapted from: Internetworldstats.com

ANALYZE THE DATA

1. Which graph makes it easier to see how the data are clustered? _____

2. Which graph makes it easier to see differences among countries? _____

3. Compare the circle graph to the one on page 35. Is population a good way to predict Internet use? Explain.

   _____

   _____

4. Which graphs would you use if you wanted to convince the government of Brazil to hook up schools and libraries to the Internet?

   _____

   _____

Comparing a Circle Graph and a Histogram

Title: _____

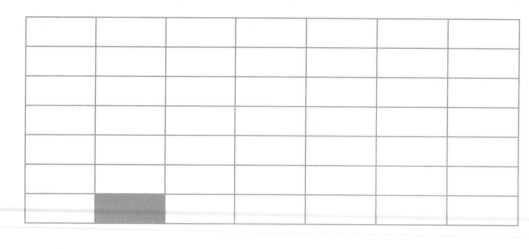

Italy

Title: _____

NUMBER AND OPERATIONS

Use the number line to help you answer each question. ◄1–5. MOC 136

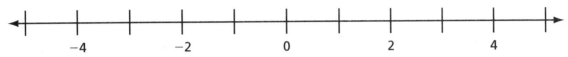

1. What are the direction and distance from −2 to 3? _____

2. Write a subtraction equation for Problem 1. _____

3. $-3 - (-2) =$ _____

4. $-2 - (-3) =$ _____

5. $-3 - (-3) =$ _____

PATTERNS AND ALGEBRA

Complete the table and write the rules. ◄6–10. MOC 136

	1	−3
	2	−6
	3	−9
6.	4	
7.	5	
8.	6	

9. Write a subtraction rule for finding a term if you know the previous term.

   _____

10. Write an addition rule for finding a term if you know the previous term.

    _____

GEOMETRY AND MEASUREMENT

Solve. ◄ 11–12. MOC 318–320, 13. MOC 366

11. Draw a coordinate grid. Label the *x*- and *y*-axes.
    Label and connect these points in order: $(-3, 0)$,
    $(-3, 4)$, $(2, 4)$, $(2, 0)$, and $(-3, 0)$.

12. Name the figure you drew in Problem 11.

    _____

13. What is the area of the figure? _____

REVIEW

Use mental math. ◄ 14–19. MOC 088–091, 116–119

14. $99 + 56 =$ _____

15. $201 - 155 =$ _____

16. $999 + 121 =$ _____

17. $10,001 - 500 =$ _____

18. $0.9 + 0.6 =$ _____

19. $1.1 - 0.5 =$ _____

Answer the question. ◄ 20–26. MOC 026

20. A dime is what percent of a dollar? _____

21. A quarter is what percent of a dollar? _____

22. A penny is what percent of a dollar? _____

23. A nickel is what percent of a dollar? _____

24. Three quarters is what percent of a dollar? _____

25. Seventy-three cents is what percent of a dollar? _____

26. Twelve dimes is what percent of a dollar? _____

GLOSSARY TO GO

Write definitions and draw pictures illustrating new math terms. The vocabulary
should be covered in your class time, so you should be familiar with most of
the terms.

Find the Alien Space Ships

Object: Find all 3 of the other player's space ships by naming coordinates on which they are located.

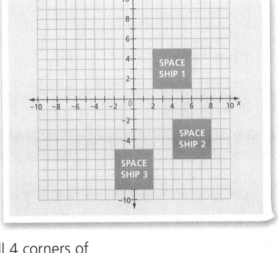

MATERIALS

Find the Alien Space Ships Pieces, pencils, paper, tall book

DIRECTIONS

1. Choose your grid and ship color. Sit across from each other with grids in front of you. Place the book so you can't see your partner's grid.

2. Place your 3 space ships anywhere on your grid. All 4 corners of each space ship must be at a point that can be named with an ordered pair of whole numbers.

3. Take turns. When you name an ordered pair, your partner tells you whether a space ship either is covering that point or has an edge or a corner on that point. If the ordered pair is not under a spaceship, your partner gives you one **clue** about what to add to one of the coordinates to get closer. **(Add −2 to the *x*-coordinate.)**

4. Keep track of the information you receive in each turn so you can narrow down the location of each space ship.

5. If you are first to name one point inside each of your partner's space ships, you win.

No hit.
Add −2 to the x-coordinate and you will be on the edge of one ship.

I guess point (3, −5).

PROBLEM SOLVING

Problem Solving: Mystery Integers

DIRECTIONS

- Rewrite the problem in your own words.

- Show your work and write the answer. Circle the strategies you used.

POSSIBLE STRATEGIES

- Guess, Check, and Revise

- Use Logical Reasoning

- Other _____

PROBLEM 1

In the following equations, each letter stands for a different integer. What integer does each letter stand for?

_____

$a + b = b$

$b + b = -4$

$a - c = 4$

PROBLEM 2

In the following equations, each letter stands for a different integer. What integer does each letter stand for?

_____

$d + e = e$

$e + e = -2$

$f - e = -2$

ANALYZE YOUR WORK

1. Did your work on the first problem help you with the second problem? If so, how?

   _____

   _____

2. Do you think there could be more than one solution to Problem 1? Explain.

   _____

   _____

Name _____

NUMBER AND OPERATIONS

Compare. Use <, >, or =. ◀1–3. MOC 046

1. −5 ◯ 6

2. −5 ◯ −6

3. −5 ◯ 0

Complete the equations. ◀4–9. MOC 136, 164

4. −5 + (−5) = _____

5. 5 + _____ = 0

6. 5 − (−5) = _____

7. −5 − (−5) = _____

8. −5 × 5 = _____

9. −5 × _____ = 25

PATTERNS AND ALGEBRA

Complete the multiplication table then answer the related question. ◀10–12. MOC 164

	×	−4	−3	−2	−1	1	2	3	4
10.	**−5**	20					−10		
11.	**4**	−16							

12. What patterns do you use to help you place the sign on the product of integers?

_____

_____

Solve the related problems. ◀13–14. MOC 108, 164, 15. MOC 048, 16. MOC 136

13. Two teams are playing a game of knowledge. A team gets 7 points for each correct answer and loses 5 points for each incorrect answer. If Team 1 answers 5 questions correctly and 3 questions incorrectly, what is their score?

_____

14. If Team 2 answers 6 questions correctly and 2 questions incorrectly, what is their score?

_____

15. Who wins the game? _____

16. How many more points did the winning team have? _____

GEOMETRY AND MEASUREMENT

Use the blank grid. ◄17. MOC 318–320, 18. MOC 363

17. Draw a coordinate grid. Label the *x*- and *y*-axes. Label and connect these points in order: (−3, 1), (−3, −2), (0, −2), (0, 1), and (−3, 1).

18. Name the quadrilateral formed by the points in Problem 17.

_____

REVIEW

Use mental math. ◄19–21. MOC 102, 106–107, 22–23. MOC 158–159

19. $\frac{1}{5} + \frac{1}{10} + \frac{2}{3} + \frac{9}{10} + \frac{4}{5} =$ _____

20. $\frac{1}{2} + \frac{3}{4} + \frac{3}{8} =$ _____

21. $0.7 + 1.5 + 0.3 + 0.04 =$ _____

22. $4 \times \$20.05 =$ _____

23. $\$10.40 \div 4 =$ _____

GLOSSARY TO GO

Write definitions and draw pictures illustrating new math terms. The vocabulary should be covered in your class time, so you should be familiar with most of the terms.

Name _____

Problem Solving: More Mysteries

DIRECTIONS

- Rewrite the problem in your own words.

- Show your work and write the answer. Circle the strategies you used.

POSSIBLE STRATEGIES

- Guess, Check, and Revise

- Use Logical Reasoning

- Other _____

PROBLEM 1

In the following equations, each letter stands for a different integer. What integer does each letter stand for?

_____

$a \times b = 50$

$a + a = -10$

$b - c = 5$

PROBLEM 2

In the following equations, each letter stands for a different integer. What integer does each letter stand for?

_____

$d \times e = 6$

$d + d = -6$

$f + e = 3$

ANALYZE YOUR WORK

1. Did your work on the first problem help you with the second problem? If so, how?

   _____

   _____

2. Do you think there could be more than one solution to Problem 2? Explain.

   _____

   _____

   _____

NUMBER AND OPERATIONS

Answer each question. ◀ 1–3. MOC 046–047

1. Name the integers greater than −4 and less than 2. _____

2. Explain why this graph does not describe Exercise 1.

_____

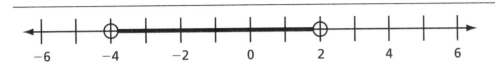

3. Explain why this graph does not describe Exercise 1.

_____

Write the missing numbers. ◀ 4–11. MOC 164

4. $-10 \times (-2) =$ _____

5. $-10 \times (-2) \times (-2) =$ _____

6. $10 \times (-10) =$ _____

7. _____ $\times (-10) = -20$

8. $-4 \times$ _____ $\times (-10) = -80$

9. $-4 \times$ _____ $\times (-10) = 80$

10. $-2 \times$ _____ $\times (-10) \times (-10) = -400$

11. $-2 \times 2 \times (-10) \times$ _____ $= 400$

PATTERNS AND ALGEBRA

Complete the table. ◀ 12–14. MOC 164

	Term	Value
	1	−20
	2	−40
	3	−60
12.	4	
13.	10	
14.	n	

GEOMETRY AND MEASUREMENT

Use the blank grid. ◀15. MOC 318–320, 16–17. MOC 363

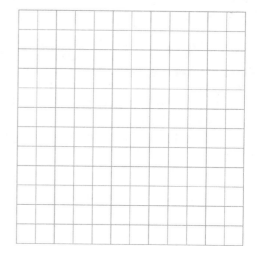

15. Draw a coordinate grid. Label the *x*- and *y*-axes. Label and connect these points in order: (2, −2), (−2, −2), (−1, 3), (2, 3), and (2, −2).

16. Name the quadrilateral formed. _____

17. Compare your figure to the one on today's Geometry Recording Pad. How is yours different?

_____

_____

REVIEW

Draw a coordinate grid then answer the related questions. ◀18–19. MOC 318–320, 20. MOC 389

18. Locate these points and connect them in order: (2, −3), (2, −7), (9, −7), (9, 6), (8, 6), (8, 5), (7, 5), (7, 10), (9, 9), (7, 8), (7, 6), (6, 6), (6, 5), (5, 5), (5, 6), (4, 6), (4, 1), (2, 1), (2, 4), (1, 3), (0, 4), (−1, 3), (−2, 4), (−2, 1), (−4, 1), (−4, 6), (−5, 6), (−5, 5), (−6, 5), (−6, 6), (−7, 6), (−7, 10), (−9, 9), (−7, 8), (−7, 5),(−8, 5), (−8, 6), (−9, 6), (−9, −7), (−2, −7), (−2, −3), (2, −3)

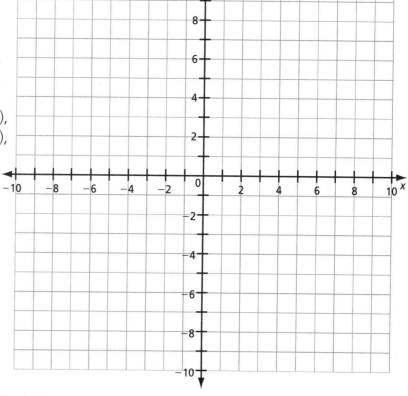

19. Describe what you see.

_____

20. Where is the line of symmetry?

_____

GLOSSARY TO GO

Review the definitions and illustrations you added to your Glossary this week. Make additions or corrections if you need to.

Name _____

Problem Solving: The Mystery Continues

DIRECTIONS

- Rewrite the problem in your own words.

- Show your work and write the answer. Circle the strategies you used.

PROBLEM 1

I am a number greater than $-1,200$ and less than -800. Some of my factors are -10, 40, and 25. What number am I?

_____

PROBLEM 2

I am a number less than -600 and greater than -900. Some of my factors are -20, 30, and 14. What number am I?

_____

ANALYZE YOUR WORK

1. If the mystery number in Problem 1 was an integer greater than or equal to $-1,200$ and less than or equal to -800, would this have changed your answer? Explain.

_____

_____

2. Would your answer be different if the mystery number in Problem 2 was an integer greater than or equal to -900 and less than or equal to -600? Explain.

_____

Summer Success: Math

This week, your child has been working with negative numbers. These are found in the real world in winter temperatures, below sea-level elevations, and accounting.

One part of the summer's work is to review vocabulary, since understanding the words is a big part of understanding how to solve problems. When you're out with your child, encourage the use of precise language by making a game out of challenging each other to describe things in detail:

Challenge your child to use these words in everyday speech.

adjacent

congruent

integer

kite

negative

parallel

quadrilateral

symmetry

On the back of this page is a word search that will let your child show off his or her vocabulary skills.

 Enjoy your time with your child, and thank you for helping to strengthen your child's comfort with important math concepts.

Word Search

There are 17 math terms in this grid. Can you find all of them?

i	n	t	e	g	e	r	c	o	d	d	f	y	e
o	u	e	q	o	p	p	o	s	i	t	e	s	l
r	m	n	u	r	o	f	m	y	s	o	r	i	e
i	b	t	a	d	i	l	p	b	t	l	p	x	n
g	e	h	l	e	n	p	a	r	a	l	l	e	l
i	r	s	a	r	t	c	r	a	n	a	o	r	t
n	o	a	x	e	s	t	e	n	c	r	t	s	h
c	o	o	r	d	i	n	a	t	e	g	r	i	d
u	n	i	t	s	y	n	e	g	a	t	i	v	e

 It might be interesting to work with your child to create another word search. If you talk about the words as you write them, you'll be helping to strengthen his or her math vocabulary.

PRACTICE TODAY'S NUMBER **24**

Name _____

NUMBER AND OPERATIONS

Answer each question. ◄1. MOC 056, 2. MOC 061

1. What are the factors of 24? _____

2. What is the prime factorization of 24? _____

Fill in the blank. ◄3–5. MOC 032

3. _____ eggs are in $\frac{1}{3}$ of 2 dozen.

4. _____ eggs are in $\frac{5}{12}$ of 2 dozen.

5. _____ eggs are in $\frac{3}{4}$ of 2 dozen.

PATTERNS AND ALGEBRA

Use the diagram to answer the questions. ◄6–7. MOC 549

6. What is the rule for finding the perimeter of figures in this pattern?

   _____

   _____

Diagram	□	⊞	⊞	⊞
Figure	1	2	3	4

7. What will be the perimeter of Figure 10? _____

GEOMETRY AND MEASUREMENT

Use your work in problem 8 to solve problem 9. ◄8. MOC 320, 353, 9. MOC 388

8. Label and connect in order points (0, 0), (−2, −3), (0, −3), and (0, 0). Name the figure you have drawn as specifically as you can.

   _____

9. Draw and label a reflection of the figure across the *x*-axis.

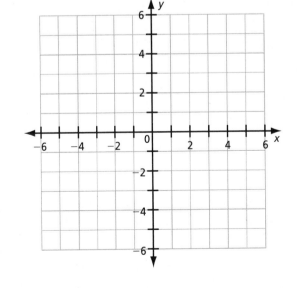

© Great Source. Permission is granted to copy this page.

SUMMER SUCCESS: MATH **79** MOC: *Math on Call*

Fill in the table and use it to solve the problems. ◄ 10–11. MOC 063–064

10. Interesting patterns come up when you add all of the factors of a number except the number itself. Prime numbers have a factor sum of 1. Circle the prime numbers. Abundant numbers have a factor sum greater than the number. Box the abundant numbers. Deficient (or defective) numbers have a factor sum less than the number. Cross out the deficient numbers.

Number	Factors	Sum of Factors Other Than the Number Itself
2	1, 2	1
3	1, 3	1
4	1, 2, 4	3
5		
6		
7		
8		
9		
10		
11		
12		
13		
14		
15		

11. Study the table. Why do you think 6 is called a perfect number?

_____

GLOSSARY TO GO

Write definitions and draw pictures illustrating new math terms. The vocabulary should be covered in your class time, so you should be familiar with most of the terms.

Factor This

Object: Create 2-digit deficient numbers.

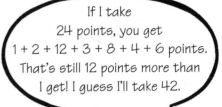

If I take 24 points, you get 1 + 2 + 12 + 3 + 8 + 4 + 6 points. That's still 12 points more than I get! I guess I'll take 42.

MATERIALS

One 1–6 number cube, one 4–9 number cube, pencils

DIRECTIONS

1. If you are Player 2, turn to page 82. You will both use this recording sheet.

2. Take turns rolling both number cubes. Use the digits to make a 2-digit number. Figure out your points this way:

Type of Number	Your Points	Partner's Points
Prime	1	1
Not Prime	Number	Sum of all factors except number

3. Record points after each turn. **Explain** how you decided what number to make. **(I rolled 2 and 4. If I take 42 points, you get 1 + 2 + 21 + 3 + 14 + 6 + 7 points. You'll get 12 more points than I will!)**

4. If you have more points after 10 rounds, you win.

= player who rolled the cubes

Round	Number	Factors Except Number	Player 1 Points	Player 2 Points
1	13	1	1	1
2	42	1, 2, 21, 3, 14, 6, 7	54	42
3				

Factor This Recording Sheet

[gray box] = player who rolled the cubes

Round	Number	Factors Except Number	Player 1 Points	Player 2 Points
1				
2				
3				
4				
5				
6				
7				
8				
9				
10				
		Sum		

[gray box] = player who rolled the cubes

Round	Number	Factors Except Number	Player 1 Points	Player 2 Points
1				
2				
3				
4				
5				
6				
7				
8				
9				
10				
		Sum		

Name _____

Making a Line Graph

How did voter turnout by 18–24 year-olds vary in national elections from 1992 through 2004?

DIRECTIONS

- Work with a partner.

- Decide on the scale and interval for the line graph on the next page.

- Title your graph and graph the data for 18–24 year-olds.

- Answer the questions to analyze the data.

National Election Voter Turnout

Year	Voter Turnout (percent) 18–24 year-olds	25–44 year-olds
1992	43	58
1994	20	39
1996	32	49
1998	17	35
2000	32	50
2002	17	34
2004	42	52

Source: www.census.gov

ANALYZE THE DATA

1. Between which 2 elections was the greatest increase in voter turnout?

   _____

   The greatest decrease? _____

2. Describe any trends or patterns you see in the data. Explain why you think that occurred.

   _____

   _____

   _____

3. If this table contained 2006 data, what would it look like? Explain your answer.

   _____

   _____

Making a Line Graph

Title: _____

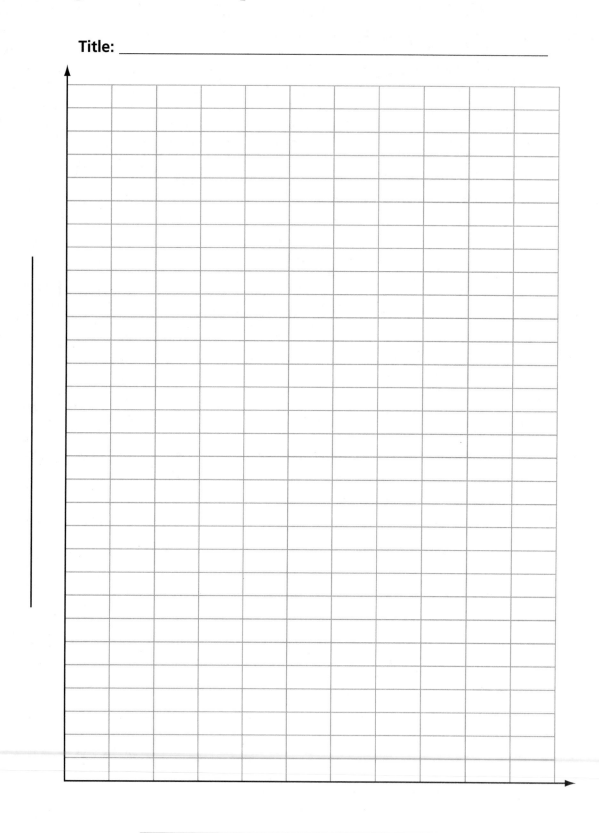

_____

Name _____

NUMBER AND OPERATIONS

Answer each question. ◀1. MOC 056, 2. MOC 061, 3. MOC 068

1. What are the factors of 36? _____

2. What is the prime factorization of 36? _____

3. What is the least common multiple of 27 and 36? Show your work._____

PATTERNS AND ALGEBRA

Use the diagram to answer the questions. ◀4–5. MOC 549

4. How many circles will be in Figure 4? _____

5. How many circles will be in Figure 6? Show your work.

_____

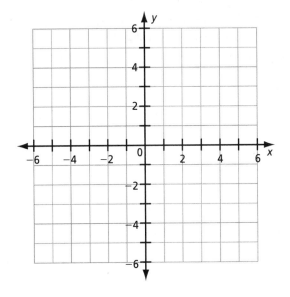

Diagram	○	○ ○ ○	○ ○ ○ ○ ○ ○
Figure	1	2	3

GEOMETRY AND MEASUREMENT

Use your work on problem 6 to solve problem 7. ◀6. MOC 320, 7. MOC 353

6. Label and connect in order points $(-4, -2)$, $(-5, 2)$, $(-4, 4)$, and $(-4, -2)$. Name the figure you have drawn as specifically as you can.

_____

7. Draw and label the reflection of the figure across the *y*-axis.

Use your work on problem 8 to answer problem 9. ◄8–9 MOC 062–064

8. Fill in the table. Circle the prime numbers. Box the abundant numbers. Cross out the deficient numbers.

Number	Factors	Sum of Factors Other Than the Number Itself
22	1, 2, 11, 22	14
23	1, 23	1
24	1, 2, 3, 4, 6, 8, 12, 24	36
25		
26		
27		
28		
29		
30		
31		

9. Is there a perfect number in the list? _____

GLOSSARY TO GO

Write definitions and draw pictures illustrating new math terms. The vocabulary should be covered in your class time, so you should be familiar with most of the terms.

Making a Double-Line Graph

How did voter turnout by 18–24 year-olds compare to the turnout
by 25–44 year-olds in national elections from 1992 to 2004?

DIRECTIONS

- Work with a partner.

- Decide on the scale and interval for the double-line graph on the next page.

- Title your graph and graph the data for both age groups.

- Write a key that explains what each line in the graph represents.

- Answer the questions to analyze the data.

National Election Voter Turnout

Year	Voter Turnout (percent) 18–24 year-olds	25–44 year-olds
1992	43	58
1994	20	39
1996	32	49
1998	17	35
2000	32	50
2002	17	34
2004	42	52

Source: www.census.gov

ANALYZE THE DATA

1. How do the periods of greatest increase and greatest decrease compare between the 2 age groups.

   _____

2. How did the turnout by the older age group compare over the years to the turnout by the younger age group?

   _____

   _____

3. If the turnout by the younger group in 2006 is 21%, what do you expect the turnout by the older age group to be? Explain your answer.

   _____

   _____

Making a Double-Line Graph

Title: _____

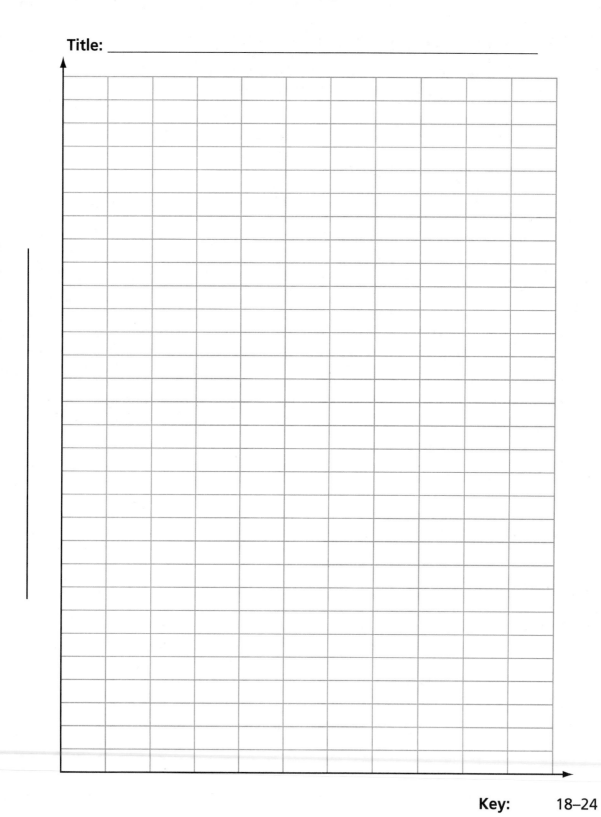

Key: 18–24

25–44

NUMBER AND OPERATIONS

Write the value of each expression. ◄1–8. MOC 071, 209

1. 2^2 _____

2. 5^2 _____

3. 15^2 _____

4. $2^2 \times 4^2 =$ _____

5. $(5 + 5) \times (2 + 2) =$ _____

6. $(5 \times 5) \times (2 \times 2) =$ _____

7. $5^2 \times 10$ _____

8. $6^2 \times 10^2$ _____

PATTERNS AND ALGEBRA

Fill in the table. Then answer the related question. ◄9–13. MOC 491

	Three Consecutive Numbers	Middle Number Squared	First Number × Third Number	Column 2 − Column 3
9.	2, 3, 4	$3^2 =$	$2 \times 4 =$	1
10.	4, 5, 6	$5^2 =$	$4 \times 6 =$	
11.	10, 11, 12	$11^2 =$	$10 \times 12 =$	
12.	99, 100, 101	$100^2 =$	$99 \times 101 =$	

13. How can you use the fact that $25^2 = 625$ to find 24×26?

_____

GEOMETRY AND MEASUREMENT

Use the diagram to answer the questions. Use 3.14 for π. ◄14–16. MOC 372–373

14. What is the length of the diameter? _____

15. What is the exact circumference? _____

16. What is the circumference to the nearest tenth of a unit?

_____

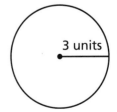

3 units

REVIEW

Use mental math to compute. ◀ 17–22. MOC 143–148, 23–28. MOC 173–175

17. 7 × 7 _____

18. 8 × 9 _____

19. 9 × 6 _____

20. 10 × 17 _____

21. 10 × 170 _____

22. 100 × 1,700 _____

23. 81 ÷ 9 _____

24. 56 ÷ 7 _____

25. 64 ÷ 8 _____

26. 5,200 ÷ 10 _____

27. 60,060 ÷ 10 _____

28. 450 ÷ 100 _____

GLOSSARY TO GO

Write definitions and draw pictures illustrating new math terms. The vocabulary should be covered in your class time, so you should be familiar with most of the terms.

Exponent Race

Object: Make and evaluate exponential expressions to cover a path across the Game Board.

MATERIALS

Exponent Race Game Board; counters: 10 each of 2 colors; two 1–6 number cubes; paper, pencils

DIRECTIONS

1. Decide which counter color will mark your plays.

2. Take turns rolling both number cubes. Use the digits to make an exponential expression. Place a counter on the Game Board to cover any square with a value equal to the expression. **Explain your choice. (Since 3⁴ is 81 and 4³ is 64, I could use either expression. I think 81 gets me closer to completing my path.)**

3. If your value is already covered, you lose your turn. If you roll 2 sixes or a 5 and 6 you can cover a *Free* spot.

4. If you are first to make a path of counters from top to bottom, you win. A path has counters in squares that touch on a side or a vertex.

I know that
$3^4 = 3^2 \times 3^2$; 3^2 is 9
and $3^2 \times 3^2$ is 9 x 9 or 81.
I'll cover 81.

1	2	3	4	5	6
8	9	16	25	27	32
36	64	64	81	125	216
243	256	625	1,024	1,296	3,125
4,096	Free	729	16	64	Free

Name _____

Problem Solving: Dollars and Friends

DIRECTIONS

- Rewrite the problem in your own words.

- Solve the problem. Circle the strategies you use.

- Show your work and write the answer.

PROBLEM 1

You give some friends $6 each. If, instead, you had given them $8 each, it would have cost you $36 more. How many friends are there?

_____

PROBLEM 2

You give some friends $8 each. If, instead, you had given them $12 each, it would have cost you $24 more. How many friends are there?

_____

ANALYZE YOUR WORK

1. Did your work on the first problem help you with the second problem? If so, how?

   _____

   _____

2. For Problem 1, change the amount in the first sentence to $5. How does that change your solution?

   _____

   _____

NUMBER AND OPERATIONS

Write the value of each expression. ◀1–6. MOC 006, 207–209

1. 10^3 _____

2. 10^4 _____

3. $10 + 10 \times 10 \times 10 =$ _____

4. $(10 + 10) \times 10 \times 10 =$ _____

5. $10^3 \times 10^4$ _____

6. $10^6 \div 10^3$ _____

PATTERNS AND ALGEBRA

Complete the table. Then answer the related question. ◀7–11. MOC 006

	Number	Number Squared	Value of Number Squared	Value as a Power of 10
7.	10	10^2		10^2
8.	100	100^2		10^4
9.	1,000			10^6
10.	10,000			10^8

11. How many zeros does the value of $1,000,000^2$ have? How did you find your answer?

_____

_____

GEOMETRY AND MEASUREMENT

Use the diagram to answer the questions. Use 3.14 for π. ◀12–17. MOC 372–375

12. What is the length of the diameter? _____

13. What is the exact circumference? _____

14. What is the circumference to the nearest tenth of an inch? _____

15. What is the exact area? _____

16. What is the area to the nearest tenth of a square inch? _____

17. What is the measure of arc AB? _____

REVIEW

Fill in the table. ◀ 18–32. MOC 071

	n	n^2
18.	2	
19.	3	
20.	4	
21.	5	
22.	6	
23.	7	
24.	8	
25.	9	
26.	10	
27.	11	
28.	12	
29.	13	
30.	14	
31.	15	
32.	16	

GLOSSARY TO GO

Write definitions and draw pictures illustrating new math terms. The vocabulary should be covered in your class time, so you should be familiar with most of the terms.

Name _____

Problem Solving: Buying Things

DIRECTIONS

- Rewrite the problem in your own words.
- Solve the problem. Circle the strategies you use.
- Show your work and complete the answer.

PROBLEM 1

Matilda bought supplies for the classroom. Scissors are $5 each and tape dispensers are $8 each. She spent $49 before tax. How many of each item did she buy?

_____

PROBLEM 2

Gus bought T-shirts for a school club. Printed T-shirts cost $12 and solid color T-shirts cost $11. He spent $116 before tax. How many of each kind of T-shirt did he buy?

_____

ANALYZE YOUR WORK

1. Did your work on the first problem help you with the second problem? If so, how?

   _____

   _____

2. Is there another solution to Problem 2?

   _____

Name _____

NUMBER AND OPERATIONS

Answer each question. ◄1–2. MOC 056, 3–4. MOC 061, 5. MOC 068

1. What are the factors of 60? _____

2. What are the factors of 16? _____

3. What is the prime factorization of 60? _____

4. What is the prime factorization of 16? _____

5. What is the least common multiple of 16 and 60? _____

Complete the ratio table and answer the question. ◄6–7. MOC 186

6. ratio: $\frac{60}{0.15}$

60		
0.15	15	

×100   ÷15

7. What is 60 ÷ 0.15? _____

PATTERNS AND ALGEBRA

Use the diagram to answer the questions. ◄8–9. MOC 316, 321

8. How many lines connect 7 points? _____

9. How many lines connect 9 points? _____

GEOMETRY AND MEASUREMENT

Use your work on problem 10 to solve problems 11 and 12. ◄10. MOC 320, 353 11. MOC 353, 388, 12. MOC 356

10. Label and connect in order points (−2, 0), (−3, 2), (−2, 4) and (−2, 0). Name the figure you have drawn as specifically as you can.

    _____

11. Draw and label the reflection of the figure across the *y*-axis.

12. What is the area of either triangle?

    _____

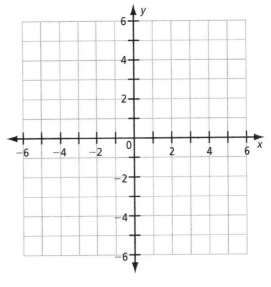

Fill in the table. Look for patterns. ◄13–29. MOC 026, 044

	Fraction	Decimal	Percent
13.	$\frac{1}{2}$		
14.	$\frac{1}{4}$		
15.	$\frac{1}{8}$		
16.	$\frac{3}{8}$		
17.	$\frac{5}{8}$		
18.	$\frac{3}{4}$		
19.	$\frac{7}{8}$		
20.	$\frac{1}{3}$		
21.	$\frac{1}{6}$		
22.	$\frac{2}{3}$		
23.	$\frac{5}{6}$		
24.	$\frac{1}{5}$		
25.	$\frac{1}{10}$		
26.	$\frac{1}{9}$		
27.	$\frac{2}{9}$		
28.	$\frac{3}{9}$		
29.	$\frac{4}{9}$		

GLOSSARY TO GO

Review the definitions and illustrations you added to your Glossary this week.
Make additions or corrections if you need to.

Name _____

Problem Solving: Oranges and Friends

DIRECTIONS

- Rewrite the problem in your own words.
- Solve the problem. Circle the strategies you use.
- Show your work.

PROBLEM 1

You give some friends 20 oranges each. If, instead, you gave each of them $\frac{9}{10}$ of 20 oranges, you would have 20 oranges left for yourself. How many friends are there?

_____

PROBLEM 2

You give some friends 48 oranges each. If, instead, you gave each of them $\frac{7}{8}$ of 48 oranges, you would have 72 oranges left for yourself. How many friends are there?

_____

ANALYZE YOUR WORK

1. Did your work on the first problem help you with the second problem? If so, how?

_____

_____

2. What math knowledge do you need to solve these problems?

_____

NEWSLETTER

Summer Success: Math

This week, students studied how numbers work. They reviewed factors, multiples, exponents, and ratios. They also studied circles, triangles, and how right triangles are related to rectangles. Finally, they learned about similarity: the relationship of figures with the same shape and different sizes.

You can help your child get comfortable with ratios while you're out shopping together. Look for items that are on sale in groups: cat food at 3 cans for $1.00, juice boxes at 6 for $3.25, and so forth. Have your child tell you how he or she can find the price of one item or 5 items.

On the back of this page is a game you can play with your child. If the numbers on 2 cards are equal ratios, the cards are a match.

 Thank you for talking with your child about math. Enjoy your time together.

Play Concentration

- Cut out the cards or copy them on index cards.

- Shuffle them and place them facedown in a 3 × 4 array.

- Take turns turning over 2 cards.

- If the numbers on your cards are equal, keep them and take another turn. Otherwise, turn them back over and let your partner take a turn.

$\frac{1}{3}$	$\frac{4}{12}$	$\frac{2}{5}$	$\frac{8}{20}$
$\frac{12\frac{1}{2}}{100}$	$\frac{125}{1,000}$	$\frac{24}{0.6}$	$\frac{40}{1}$
$\frac{5}{6}$	$\frac{50}{60}$	$\frac{2}{3}$	$\frac{66\frac{2}{3}}{100}$

Enjoy these activities with your child. Remember that using math in the real world helps your child understand that math is important in school.

Name _____

NUMBER AND OPERATIONS

Complete the table. Then plot the points on the coordinate grid and connect the points. ◄1. MOC 243, 245–247

1. $y = 2x$

x	y
0	
1	
2	
4	
−1	
−2	
−3	

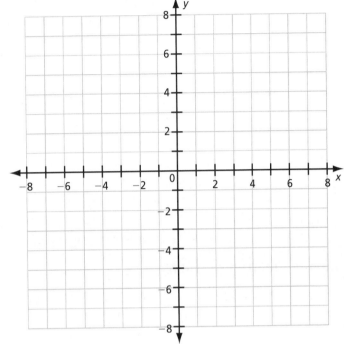

PATTERNS AND ALGEBRA

Use the diagram to solve the problems. ◄2–5. MOC 228–229

2. Write an expression to describe what is on the left side of the scale.

_____

3. Write an expression to describe what is on the right side of the scale. _____

4. Each bag holds the same number of apples and all apples weigh the same. Write an equation for the diagram.

_____

5. How can you find the number of apples in a bag?

_____

_____

GEOMETRY AND MEASUREMENT

Use the diagram of the cube to answer the questions. ◄6–8. MOC 399–401

6. How many faces? _____

7. Each face is the shape of what polygon? _____

8. What is the total area of the faces of the cube? _____

2 cm

REVIEW

For each phrase, write an algebraic expression using *x* as the variable. ◄9–12. MOC 204

9. 5 more than a number: _____

10. 4 times a number: _____

11. 3 less than a number: _____

12. $\frac{2}{3}$ of a number: _____

Solve these pairs of related problems. ◄13–16. MOC 203–206, 241–242

13. José wants to read a book with 539 pages in seven days. He wants to read the same number of pages each day. How many pages must he read each day? _____

14. When José has read 154 pages, what fraction of the book has he read? _____

15. Maria is reading a book with 360 pages. How many pages has she read when she has read 25% of the book?

    _____

16. How many pages has she read when she has read $33\frac{1}{3}$% of the book?

    _____

GLOSSARY TO GO

Write definitions and draw pictures illustrating new math terms. The vocabulary should be covered in your class time, so you should be familiar with most of the terms.

Terrific Triangle

Object: Plot a large triangle and find its area.

MATERIALS

Two 1–6 number cubes, ruler, pencils

DIRECTIONS

1. If you are Player 2, turn to page 106. If you are Player 1, roll the number cubes and make an ordered pair from the digits. Plot that point on your coordinate grid.

2. Take turns rolling the number cubes and plotting points until you have 3 points on your grid.

3. If possible, connect your points to make a triangle.

4. If you made a triangle, find its area to get your score. **Explain how to find your area. (My triangle sits in a 4 × 4 square. I can subtract the areas of 3 right triangles to find its area.)**

5. If your triangle's area is greater, or if your figure is the only triangle, you win the round.

The non-triangle area of my square is $\frac{1}{2}$ of 3 × 3 plus $\frac{1}{2}$ of 4 × 1 plus $\frac{1}{2}$ of 4 × 1 again. Since $16 - 8\frac{1}{2} = 7\frac{1}{2}$, my area is $7\frac{1}{2}$ square units.

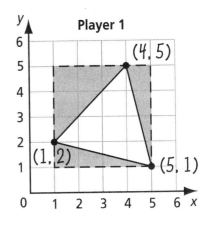

Player 1

Terrific Triangle Recording Sheet

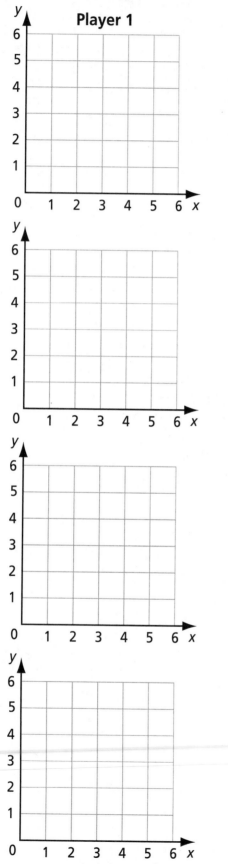

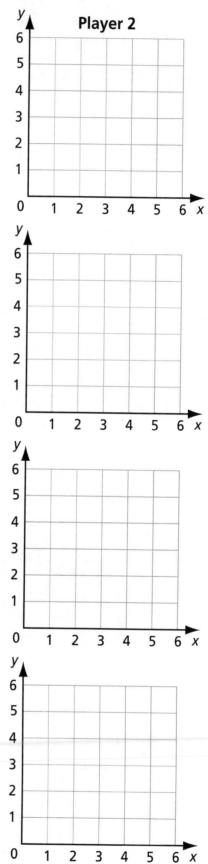

Name _____

Making a Scatter Plot

Can you use the winning time in the women's Olympic 100-meter race to predict the winning time in the 1,500-meter race?

DIRECTIONS

- Work with a partner.

- Decide on scales and intervals for both axes of the plot on the next page.

- Plot the data for distance and time and answer the questions to analyze the data.

2004 Olympic Women's Track Races

Race Distance (in meters)	Winning Time (in seconds)	Winning Average Speed (in meters per second)
100	10.93	9.15
200	22.05	9.07
400	49.41	8.10
800	116.38	6.87
1,500	237.90	6.31

Source: wikipedia.org

ANALYZE THE DATA

1. What are the ranges in race distances and winning times?

   distance: _____

   time: _____

2. If all runners could run at the 100-meter rate, what would be their times?

   200 meters: _____

   400 meters: _____

   800 meters: _____

   1,500 meters: _____

3. What conclusion can you draw from your scatter plot about whether the winning time in the 100-meter race can be used to predict the winning time in the 1,500-meter race?

   _____

   _____

Making a Scatter Plot

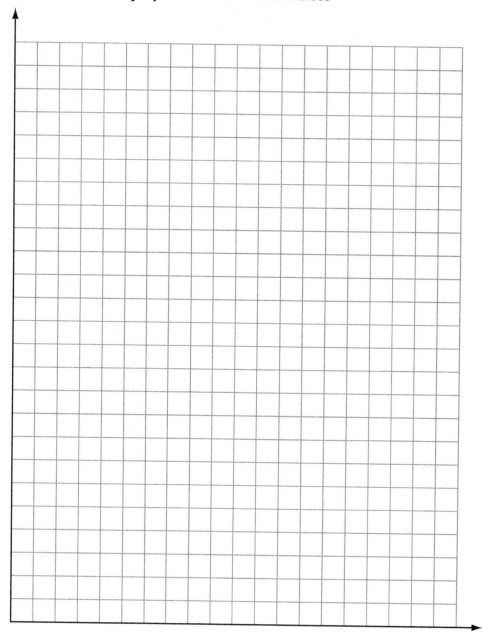

Olympic Women's Track Races

Name _____

NUMBER AND OPERATIONS

Complete each table. Then plot the points on the coordinate grid and connect the points. ◀1–2. MOC 243, 245–247

1. $y = 3x + 2$

x	y
−3	
−2	
−1	
0	
1	
2	

2. $y = 2x − 1$

x	y
−2	
−1	
0	
1	
2	
3	

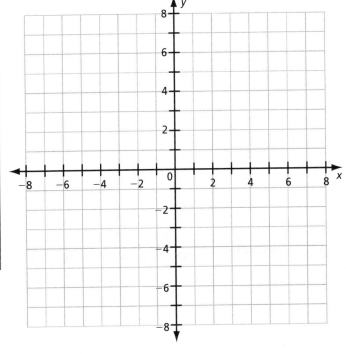

PATTERNS AND ALGEBRA

Use the diagram to solve. ◀3–6. MOC 228–229

3. What is on the left side of the balance?

_____

4. What is on the right side of the balance?

_____

5. Each bag holds the same number of apples and all apples weigh the same. Write an equation using b to mean a bag of apples to show this balance.

_____

6. Solve your equation from Problem 5 to determine how many apples are in each bag. Show your work.

GEOMETRY AND MEASUREMENT

Use the diagram of the figure to answer the questions. ◄7–11. MOC 394

7. What is the name of this figure? Be as specific as you can.

    _____

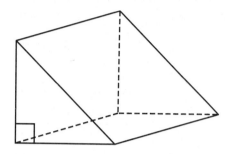

8. What shape is a base of this prism?

    _____

9. What shape are the other faces?

    _____

10. How many vertices? _____

11. How many edges? _____

REVIEW

Order the fractions on the number line. ◄12. MOC 049

12. $\frac{5}{6}, \frac{1}{4}, \frac{1}{3}, \frac{1}{6}, \frac{2}{3},$ and $\frac{1}{2}$

Solve these problems. ◄13–15. MOC 205

13. The first song on a CD is $4\frac{1}{2}$ minutes long. The second song is $3\frac{5}{6}$ minutes long. How many minutes are both songs together? Give your answer in simplest form.

    _____

14. How much longer is the first song than the second? _____

15. There are 12 songs on the CD. If the average or mean time for each song is $4\frac{1}{6}$ minutes, how many minutes of music are on the CD?

    _____

GLOSSARY TO GO

Write definitions and draw pictures illustrating new math terms. The vocabulary should be covered in your class time, so you should be familiar with most of the terms.

Name _____

Scatter Plots and Correlations

Is there a correlation between the average speed of the winners of Olympic women's races and the race distance?

DIRECTIONS

- Work with a partner.
- Decide on scales and intervals for both axes of the plot on the next page.
- Plot the data for race distance and average speed.
- Answer the questions to analyze the data.

2004 Olympic Women's Track Races

Race Distance (in meters)	Winning Time (in seconds)	Winning Average Speed (in meters per second)
100	10.93	9.15
200	22.05	9.07
400	49.41	8.10
800	116.38	6.87
1,500	237.90	6.31

Source: wikipedia.org

ANALYZE THE DATA

1. Describe the shape of the data on your scatter plot.

   _____

   _____

2. What explanation can you give for the shape of the graph?

   _____

   _____

3. For a short time the Olympics also included a women's 3,000-meter race. What would you estimate might have been a winning time and average speed for a 3,000-meter race in 2004? Explain your answer.

   _____

   _____

Scatter Plots and Correlations

Olympic Women's Track Races

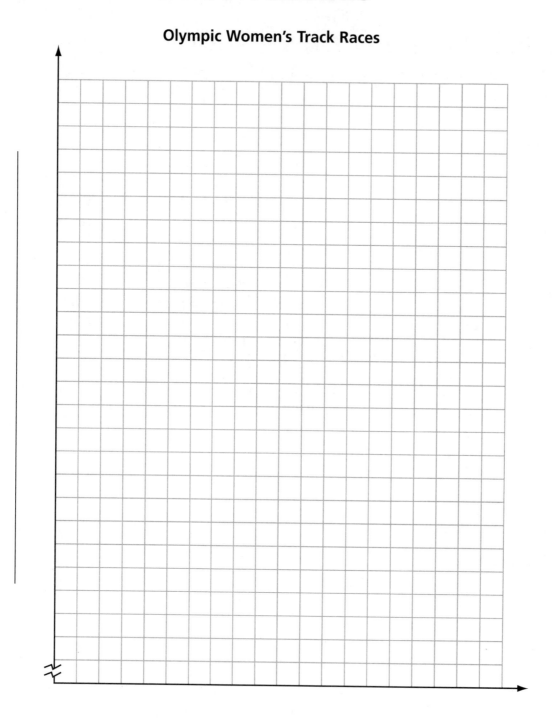

⌇ The grid lines between 0 and 5 have been removed to save space.

NUMBER AND OPERATIONS

Write each sum or difference. ◄1–2. MOC 108, 3–4. MOC 239

1. $-1 + 5 =$ _____

2. $-8 - (-6) =$ _____

3. $2x + 4x =$ _____

4. $-6x - 3x =$ _____

PATTERNS AND ALGEBRA

Solve each equation. ◄5–8. MOC 239–242

5. $2x + 1 = 9$, $x =$ _____

6. $4x + 2 = 14$, $x =$ _____

7. $7x - 3x = 8$, $x =$ _____

8. $2x = -4$, $x =$ _____

Solve the related problems. ◄9–11. MOC 243–247

9. Fill in the table of values for $y = 4x - 8$.

x	y
0	
2	
4	

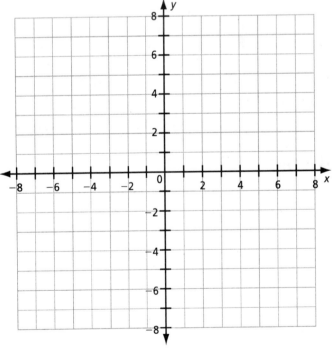

10. Plot and connect the points.

11. Show how to use the graph to find the value of x when $y = 6$.

_____

GEOMETRY AND MEASUREMENT

Use the drawing to answer the questions. ◄12–14. MOC 407

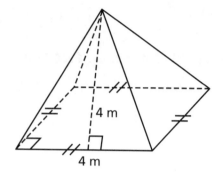

12. What is the area of the square base? _____

13. What is the area of each triangular face? _____

14. What is the surface area? _____

REVIEW

Fill in the table. ◄15–25. MOC 071

	Number (*n*)	Number Cubed (n^3)
15.	1	
16.	2	
17.	3	
18.	4	
19.	5	
20.	6	
21.	7	
22.	8	
23.	9	
24.	10	
25.	100	

GLOSSARY TO GO

Write definitions and draw pictures illustrating new math terms. The vocabulary should be covered in your class time, so you should be familiar with most of the terms.

Roll a Factor

Object: Cover 4 multiples in a row.

MATERIALS

Roll a Factor Game Board; counters: 10 each of 2 colors; a
4–9 number cube

DIRECTIONS

1. Choose the counter color that will mark your plays.

2. Take turns rolling the number cube. Place a counter on a
multiple of the number on the cube. **Explain** how you chose
your number. **(I rolled 5. I know that, if a number has 5 in
the ones place, it is a multiple of 5, so I'll mark 125.)**

3. You can place a counter in any open square. If there is no open
square you can use, you lose your turn.

4. If you are first to have 4 counters in a row horizontally, vertically,
or diagonally, you win.

I can get 2
in a row and block you if
I put a counter on the 125
in the second row.

56	63	72	42	49	64
63	44	125	56	88	120
72	125	210	360	160	288
42	56	360	640	490	144
49	88	160	490	120	44
64	120	288	144	44	77

Name _____

Problem Solving: Costs and Friends

DIRECTIONS

- Rewrite the problem in your own words.

- Solve the problem. Circle the strategies you used.

- Show your work and write the answer.

POSSIBLE STRATEGIES

- Guess, Check, and Revise

- Work Backward

- Make a Table or Organized List

- Write an Equation

- Make a Model or a Diagram

- Other _____

PROBLEM 1

Jake and 3 of his friends went to a restaurant. Each person ordered a turkey sandwich. Their bill for $14.21 included $1.05 sales tax. How much does one turkey sandwich cost before tax?

_____

PROBLEM 2

Latoya and 4 of her classmates went to a clothing store. Each person bought a school uniform. Their bill for $240.75 included $15.75 sales tax. How much does one school uniform cost before tax?

ANALYZE YOUR WORK

1. Did your work on the first problem help you with the second problem? If so, how?

   _____

   _____

2. What math knowledge do you need to know to solve these problems?

   _____

   _____

Name _____

NUMBER AND OPERATIONS

Complete the table of values and graph the points. ◀1. MOC 243–247

1.

x	y
−2	−8
0	−4
2	0
4	

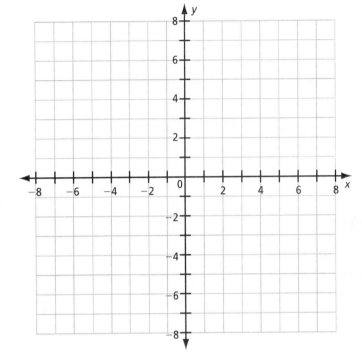

Refer to problem 1 to answer these questions. ◀2–3. MOC 248

2. As the value of *y* increases in your table of values, how does the value of *x* change?

_____

3. According to your graph, what is the value of *y* when *x* is 6? _____

PATTERNS AND ALGEBRA

Use the diagram. ◀4–7. MOC 228–229

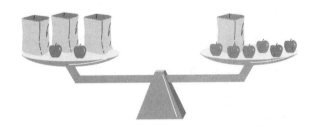

4. Write an expression to describe what is on the left side of the scale.

_____

5. Write an expression to describe what is on the right side of the scale. _____

6. Write an equation for the diagram _____

7. How can you find the number of apples in a bag?

_____

_____

GEOMETRY AND MEASUREMENT

Use the diagram to help answer the questions. ◀ 8–9. MOC 393–414

8. Label each figure.

9. How are the cone and cylinder alike and different?

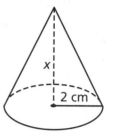 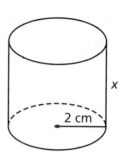

_____

_____

_____   _____   _____

_____

_____

REVIEW

Solve. ◀ 10–14. MOC 205

10. Milk, bread, and peanut butter cost $7.83. The milk costs $1.99 and the bread costs $1.89. How much does the peanut butter cost? _____

11. The refreshments for a party cost $12.65. If five friends split the cost, how much does each friend have to pay? _____

12. A pair of $40 shoes are on sale for 10% off. How much do they cost on sale? _____

13. One CD costs $13.99. What is the cost of 11 CDs? _____

14. If you save 15¢ every day in a jar, how much will you save

   A. in the month of February in a leap year? _____

   B. in the month of August? _____

   C. in one year (not a leap year)? _____

GLOSSARY TO GO

Write definitions and draw pictures illustrating new math terms. The vocabulary should be covered in your class time, so you should be familiar with most of the terms.

PROBLEM SOLVING

Name _____

Problem Solving: Cutting Up Things

DIRECTIONS

- Rewrite the problem in your own words.
- Solve the problem. Circle the strategies you use.
- Show your work and write the answer.

POSSIBLE STRATEGIES

- Guess, Check, and Revise
- Work Backward
- Make a Table or Organized List
- Write an Equation
- Make a Model or a Diagram
- Other _____

PROBLEM 1

Kevin cut a board into 2 equal pieces. Then he cut 10 inches off of one of the pieces. That piece is now 25 inches long. What was the original length of the board?

PROBLEM 2

Elena cut a piece of ribbon into 3 pieces. Then, she cut $\frac{1}{2}$ foot off one of the pieces. That piece is now 10 inches long. What was the original length of the ribbon?

ANALYZE YOUR WORK

1. Did your work on the first problem help you with the second problem? If so, how?

2. How is Problem 2 a little different than Problem 1?

SUMMER SUCCESS: MATH **119** *Math on Call 355*

NUMBER AND OPERATIONS

Complete each table. Then graph and label each function. ◀1–2. MOC 243, 247, 3–5. MOC 248

1. $x + y = 8$

x	y
1	
2	
3	

2. $x - y = 10$

x	y
8	
7	
5	

3. Look at the functions you graphed in Problems 1 and 2. Which graph goes down from left to right?

_____

4. Where do the 2 lines intersect?

_____

5. What is special about the coordinates of the point you named in Problem 4?

_____

_____

_____

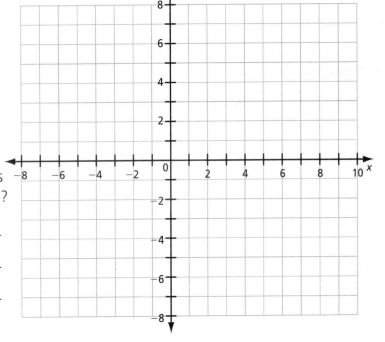

PATTERNS AND ALGEBRA

Solve. ◀6–7. MOC 205

6. Explain why x cannot have more than one value in $x + 5 = 3x + 1$.

_____

_____

7. What is the value of x? _____

GEOMETRY AND MEASUREMENT

Use the diagram. ◄8–14. MOC 394–396

8. Name the shape. _____

9. What shape is each base and how many are there?

_____

10. What is the area of each base? _____

11. What shape is each face and how many are there?

_____

12. What is the area of each face? _____

13. What is the surface area? _____

14. How many 1-inch cubes will fit in it? _____

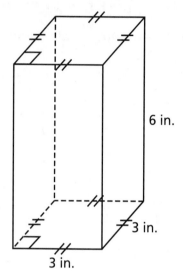

6 in.

3 in.

3 in.

REVIEW

Solve these problems. ◄15. MOC 107, 16. MOC 135, 17. MOC 162, 18–19. MOC 192, 20–21. MOC 205

15. $\frac{1}{2} + \frac{1}{4} =$ _____

16. $1 - \frac{3}{8} =$ _____

17. $\frac{1}{2} \times \frac{1}{2} =$ _____

18. $\frac{1}{2} \div \frac{1}{4} =$ _____

19. $1\frac{1}{2} \div \frac{1}{4} =$ _____

20. A costume takes $1\frac{1}{2}$ yards of material to make. You have 15 yards of material. How many costumes can you make? _____

21. How many $\frac{1}{2}$-yard pieces can you make from a 3-yard piece of material? _____

GLOSSARY TO GO

Review the definitions and illustrations you added to your Glossary this week. Make additions or corrections if you need to.

Name _____

Problem Solving: Prisms and Surface Area

DIRECTIONS

- Rewrite the problem in your own words.

- Solve the problem. Circle the strategies you use.

- Show your work and write the answer.

POSSIBLE STRATEGIES

- Guess, Check, and Revise

- Work Backward

- Make a Table or Organized List

- Write an Equation

- Make a Model or a Diagram

- Other _____

PROBLEM 1

The surface area of a rectangular prism is 162 square inches. Its side-lengths are all whole numbers. Is the prism a cube? If so, find the length of a side.

_____

PROBLEM 2

The surface area of a rectangular prism is 384 square centimeters. Its side-lengths are all whole numbers. Is the prism a cube? If so, find the length of a side.

_____

ANALYZE YOUR WORK

1. Did your work on the first problem help you with the second problem? If so, how?

   _____

   _____

2. What math knowledge do you need to solve these problems?

   _____

   _____

Summer Success: Math

This week, we solved equations in a variety of ways. We learned that solving an equation is like keeping the trays of a balance scale balanced: if you do something to one side, you must do the same thing to the other side.

On the back of this page are directions for a trick that will help your child think algebraically. Ask your child to show you why it works: Think of the original number as a number of apples hidden in a bag.

- Multiplying by 4 gives 4 bags.

- Adding 2 makes 4 bags and 2 loose apples.

- Dividing by 2 makes 2 bags and 1 loose apple.

- Subtracting the original number takes away 1 bag.

- Subtracting it again takes away the other bag, so all that's left is 1 loose apple, no matter what number of apples you started with!

 Enjoy your time with your child, and thank you for helping to strengthen your child's comfort with important math concepts.

Number Trick

Try this trick on a friend or family member. Ask the person to silently—

1. Pick a number.

2. Multiply it by 4.

3. Add 2 to the product.

4. Divide the sum by 2.

5. Subtract the original number.

6. Subtract the original number again.

Close your eyes and pretend to be concentrating very hard. Then, announce, *your final result is 1!*

Show your child that you're proud of his or her progress. Remember that using math in the real world will help your child understand that math is important in school.

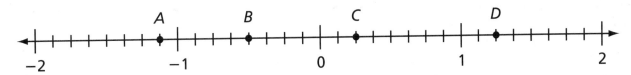

PRACTICE TODAY'S NUMBER $-\dfrac{1}{2}$

Name _____

NUMBER AND OPERATIONS

Use the number line. ◄1–5. MOC 048

```
         A        B          C            D
◄——+——+——+——●——+——+——+——●——+——+——+——●——+——+——+——●——+——+——+——►
  -2        -1          0            1            2
```

1. What is the coordinate of *B*? _____

2. Which point has a coordinate of $\frac{1}{4}$? _____

3. What is the coordinate of point *A*? _____

4. Which point has a coordinate of $\frac{5}{4}$? _____

5. Graph all points greater than $-\frac{1}{2}$ and less than $1\frac{1}{2}$. How do you use inequality symbols to write this?

   _____

Write each product. ◄6–9. MOC 071, 160–164

6. $-\frac{1}{2} \times \frac{1}{3} =$ _____

7. $-\frac{1}{2} \times 6 =$ _____

8. $-\frac{1}{2} \times \frac{1}{2} =$ _____

9. $(-\frac{1}{2})^2 =$ _____

PATTERNS AND ALGEBRA

Solve for *n*. Show your work. ◄10–13. MOC 228–229

10. $2n = -8$; $n =$ _____

11. $\frac{1}{2}n = -8$; $n =$ _____

12. $n + e = \$1.10$; $3e = \$2.10$; $n =$ _____

13. $3x = 12$; $n + x = 9$; $n =$ _____

GEOMETRY AND MEASUREMENT

Use the diagram to answer the questions.
Use 3.14 for π. ◄14. MOC 409; 15. MOC 413

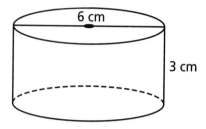

14. What is the radius of the base? _____

15. What is the exact volume of the cylinder? _____

REVIEW

Write each quotient. ◄16–23. MOC 193

16. 24 ÷ 3 = _____

17. −24 ÷ (−3) = _____

18. 12 ÷ 4 = _____

19. −12 ÷ (−4) = _____

20. 20 ÷ (−5) = _____

21. −20 ÷ 5 = _____

22. 16 ÷ (−4) = _____

23. −16 ÷ 4 = _____

GLOSSARY TO GO

Write definitions and draw pictures illustrating new math terms. The vocabulary should be covered in your class time, so you should be familiar with most of the terms.

Make That Surface

Object: Create a square prism with the greatest possible surface area.

MATERIALS

Two 1–6 number cubes, paper, pencils

DIRECTIONS

1. If you are Player 2, turn to page 130. You will both use this recording sheet.

2. Take turns rolling both number cubes. Use one number for *a* and the other for *b*.

3. On your recording sheet, write and solve an equation for the surface area. Draw a diagram if it helps. **Explain** your reasoning. **(I rolled 3 and 4. A 4 by 4 square is bigger than a 3 by 3 square, so I'll use 4 as the side of the square base.)**

4. Mark the prism with the greatest surface area for each round.

5. If your prism has greater surface area for 3 of 5 rounds, you win.

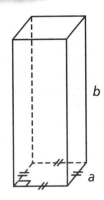

If I choose 4 for a, the area of the bases will be greater than if I choose 3. The other faces will have the same area either way.

Round		Equation	Surface Area
1	Player 1	S. A. = $(2 \times 6^2) + 4 \times (6 \times 2)$ = $(2 \times 36) + 4 \times 12$ = $72 + 48$ = 120	120 units^2
	Player 2	S. A. = $(2 \times 4^2) + 4 \times (4 \times 3)$ = $(2 \times 16) + 4 \times 12$ = $32 + 48$ = 80	80 units^2

Make That Surface Recording Sheet

Round		Equation	Surface Area
1	Player 1	S. A. =	
	Player 2	S. A. =	
2	Player 1	S. A. =	
	Player 2	S. A. =	
3	Player 1	S. A. =	
	Player 2	S. A. =	
4	Player 1	S. A. =	
	Player 2	S. A. =	
5	Player 1	S. A. =	
	Player 2	S. A. =	

Name _____

Probability of Simple Events

How can the probability of an event change?

MATERIALS

30 blue and 30 red counters, 3 paper bags

DIRECTIONS

	Counters in the Bag	
Bag	**Red**	**Blue**
A	10	10
B	5	15
C	15	5

- Work with a partner.
- Place counters in bags according to this table.
- Randomly pick one counter from each bag, tally the color, and return the counter to the bag.
- Repeat for a total of 20 picks from each bag and record the results in the chart below.
- Complete the chart. Graph the data as a double bar graph on page 132.
- Answer the questions to analyze the data.

	Picks		Probability of Picking a Red Counter	
Bag	**Red**	**Blue**	**Theoretical**	**Experimental**
A			$\frac{10}{20}$	
B			$\frac{5}{20}$	
C			$\frac{15}{20}$	

ANALYZE THE DATA

1. For which bag is the theoretical probability of picking a red counter the greatest? For which bag was the experimental probability the greatest?

   theoretical probability: _____ experimental probability: _____

2. Did the experimental probability match the theoretical probability for each bag? If not, explain why they did not match.

   _____

   _____

3. How does your graph help you see how the data compare?

   _____

Graphing Probability of Simple Events

Title: _____

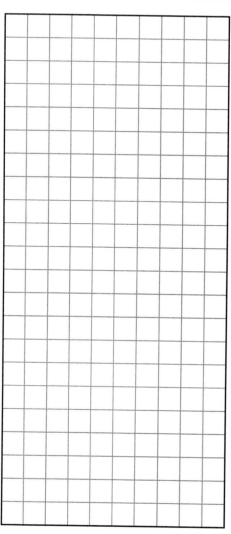

Name _____

NUMBER AND OPERATIONS

Write the value of each expression. ◄1–6. MOC 071, 7–10. MOC 207–209

1. 2^4 _____

2. 1^4 _____

3. 10^4 _____

4. 3^4 _____

5. 4^4 _____

6. 100^4 _____

7. $2 + 4 \times 5$ _____

8. $(10 - 2) \times (4 + 3)$ _____

9. $4 \div 2 + 2^4$ _____

10. $(7 - 2) \times 4 + 3$ _____

PATTERNS AND ALGEBRA

Write and solve equations for the related problems. ◄11–14. MOC 205, 239

11. Write an equation to show that 2 salads and 2 ham and cheese wraps cost $20.50.

_____

12. Solve an equation to show the cost of 1 salad and 1 ham and cheese wrap.

13. A fruit plate and a ham and cheese wrap cost $9.25. Which costs more, a fruit plate or a salad? How much more?

_____

14. Write an equation to show the relationship between the cost of a salad and the cost of a fruit plate.

_____

GEOMETRY AND MEASUREMENT

Use the diagram to answer the questions. Use 3.14 for π. ◂ 15–17. MOC 402, 413

15. Write an equation for the volume of Figure A.

_____

16. Write an equation for the volume of Figure B.

_____

17. Use your equations to write an inequality that compares the volumes of the figures.

_____

Figure A

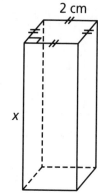

Figure B

2 cm

x

2 cm

x

REVIEW

Plot your points on the coordinate grid. ◂ 18–19. MOC 320

18. Draw a polygon with more than 6 sides. Your polygon must lie in all 4 quadrants on the grid and use only integers as coordinates.

19. List your polygon's ordered pairs so that a friend could use them to make an exact copy of your polygon.

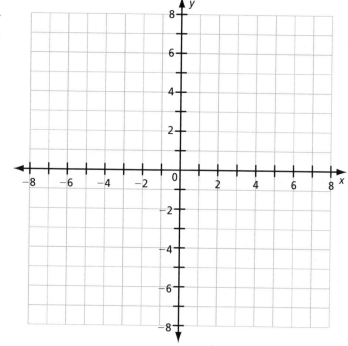

GLOSSARY TO GO

Write definitions and draw pictures illustrating new math terms. The vocabulary should be covered in your class time, so you should be familiar with most of the terms.

More Probability of Simple Events

How does probability change when the favorable event can be one of 2 possibilities?

MATERIALS

5 blue, 5 red, and 10 yellow counters; paper bag

DIRECTIONS

- Work with a partner.
- Mix 5 blue counters, 5 red counters, and 10 yellow counters in a bag.
- Pick a counter, record the color, and return the counter to the bag.
- Do 3 trials of 20 picks each.
- Answer the questions to analyze the data.

Trial	Blue	Red	Yellow	Experimental Probability of Picking Red or Blue
1				
2				
3				
Sum				

ANALYZE THE DATA

1. What is the theoretical probability that you'll pick blue? _____

   Red? _____ Yellow? _____

2. What is the theoretical probability of picking either red or blue? _____

3. How do the results of your experiment compare to the theoretical probability?

   _____

   _____

4. Name 2 things you could do to make it more likely that you will pick a red or blue counter.

   _____

   _____

NUMBER AND OPERATIONS

Write each number in standard form and word form. ◄1–4. MOC 016

1. 1.0×10^6

_____

2. 2.0×10^6

_____

3. 2.1×10^6

_____

4. 2.11×10^6

_____

Write each number using scientific notation. ◄5–6. MOC 016

5. one million _____

6. 2,400,000 _____

PATTERNS AND ALGEBRA

Write and simplify or solve equations for the related problems. ◄7–10. MOC 205

7. Write equations that describe these orders at a local pizza shop. Two subs and a bottle of flavored water cost $10.95. Three subs and a bottle of water cost $15.20.

_____

8. Write the equation you get when you combine the 2 equations by subtracting the first equation from the second.

_____

9. How much does one sub cost? _____

10. What is the cost of a bottle of water? _____

GEOMETRY AND MEASUREMENT

Use the diagram to answer the questions. Use 3.14 for π. ◄11–14. MOC 370

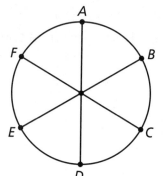

11. The circle is divided into sixths. What is the measure of each of the central angles?

    _____

12. What is the measure of arc *AC*? _____

13. What is the measure of arc *AD*? _____

14. What is the measure of arc *ACF*? _____

REVIEW

Write a fraction in simplest form to describe the shaded part of each set of triangles. ◄15–18. MOC 028

15. △▲▲ / ▲△▲

    _____

16. ▲△▲▲ ▲ / ▲▲▲△

    _____

17. ▲△△▲△ / △▲△△△

    _____

18. △▲▲ / ▲△△

    _____

Write each of these fractions as a percent. Draw and label a diagram of one of them. ◄19–22. MOC 442

19. $\frac{3}{4}$ _____

20. $\frac{2}{3}$ _____

21. $\frac{1}{8}$ _____

22. $\frac{7}{8}$ _____

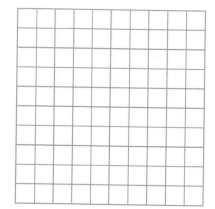

GLOSSARY TO GO

Write definitions and draw pictures illustrating new math terms. The vocabulary should be covered in your class time, so you should be familiar with most of the terms.

Solve That Equation

Object: Cover 4 numbers in a row by solving equations.

MATERIALS

Solve That Equation Game Board; counters: 10 each of 2 colors; 2 paper clips; paper; pencils

DIRECTIONS

1. Choose the counter color to mark your plays.

2. If you are Player 1, place a paper clip on an expression at the top of the Game Board. Place the other paper clip on a number at the bottom of the Game Board. Use the expression and the number to make an equation.

3. Solve the equation. **Convince** your partner that the solution is correct. **(I put one clip on $\frac{x}{2}$ and the other on 9. My equation is, half of x equals 9. If half of x equals 9, then x is 9 × 2. I can cover the 18.)** Place a counter on any free space on the Game Board that contains the value of x.

4. If you are Player 2, move just one of the paper clips to a new expression or a new number and make a new equation.

5. Take turns moving one clip, solving the equation, and covering an open square on the board.

6. If you are first to get 4 counters in a row horizontally, vertically, or diagonally, you win.

I am going to move the clip from $\frac{x}{2}$ to x^2. If a number squared is 9, then the number must be 3. That gives me 2 in a row and it blocks you.

Name _____

Problem Solving: Thinking of Integers

DIRECTIONS

- Solve the problem. Circle the strategies you used.
- Show your work.

PROBLEM 1

Two integers have a sum of 1 and a difference of 5. What are the integers?

_____

PROBLEM 2

Write and graph equations for Problem 1.

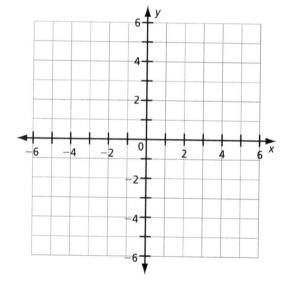

ANALYZE YOUR WORK

1. Did your work on the first problem help you with the second problem? If so, how?

   _____

   _____

2. How can you use graphs to find the solution to 2 related equations?

   _____

   _____

Name _____

NUMBER AND OPERATIONS

Write each number in scientific notation. ◀1–4. MOC 016

1. 6,400,000,000 _____

2. $2 \times 10^3 \times 6$ _____

3. $3 \times 5,880,000,000,000$ _____

4. twelve billion _____

Write each number in standard form and in word form. ◀5–6. MOC 016

5. 5.88×10^{12} _____

_____

6. $2.5 \times 10^4 \times 6.0 \times 10^8$ _____

_____

PATTERNS AND ALGEBRA

Write and solve an equation. ◀7–9. MOC 205–206

7. Compare $x + 2y$ to $3x + y$ if $x + 2y = 15$ and $3x + y = 15$.

_____

8. Simplify your answer to Problem 7 to get y by itself on one side of the equation.

_____

9. Find the value of x by substituting the value of y from Problem 8 into one of the equations from Problem 7.

MEASUREMENT

Answer the related questions. Use 3.14 for π. ◄ 10–12. MOC 375

10. What is the area to the nearest hundredth of the smaller circle?

_____

11. What is the area to the nearest hundredth of the larger circle?

_____

12. What is the area to the nearest hundredth of the shaded region?

_____

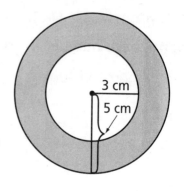

REVIEW

Solve each problem. ◄ 13–21. MOC 536

13. How many eggs are in $\frac{1}{3}$ of a dozen? _____

14. How many inches are in $\frac{1}{6}$ of a foot? _____

15. How many inches are in $2\frac{1}{2}$ feet? _____

16. How many quarts are in $\frac{3}{4}$ of a gallon? _____

17. How many ounces are in $\frac{1}{2}$ of a pound? _____

18. What fraction of a pound is 4 ounces? _____

19. What fraction of a dozen is 8? _____

20. What fraction of a yard is 18 inches? _____

21. What fraction of a dozen is 10? _____

GLOSSARY TO GO

Write definitions and draw pictures illustrating new math terms. The vocabulary should be covered in your class time, so you should be familiar with most of the terms.

Name _____

Problem Solving: More Dimensions

DIRECTIONS

- Solve the problem. Circle the strategies you used.
- Show your work. Don't forget to use units.

POSSIBLE STRATEGIES

- Guess, Check, and Revise
- Make a Table or an Organized List
- Make a Model or Diagram
- Make a Graph
- Other _____

PROBLEM 1

Half the perimeter of a rectangle is 14 centimeters. The area of the rectangle is 24 square centimeters. The dimensions are whole numbers. What are they?

_____

PROBLEM 2

Half the perimeter of a rectangle is 22 centimeters. The area of the rectangle is 72 square centimeters. The dimensions are whole numbers. What are they?

_____

ANALYZE YOUR WORK

Think about how you have used graphs to help solve problems.

- **A.** Write equations for Problem 1. _____
- **B.** Fill in the tables of values for your equations on page 144.
- **C.** Graph the equations.
- **D.** How can a graph help you find the common solution for the 2 equations?

_____

_____

Problem Solving: More Dimensions

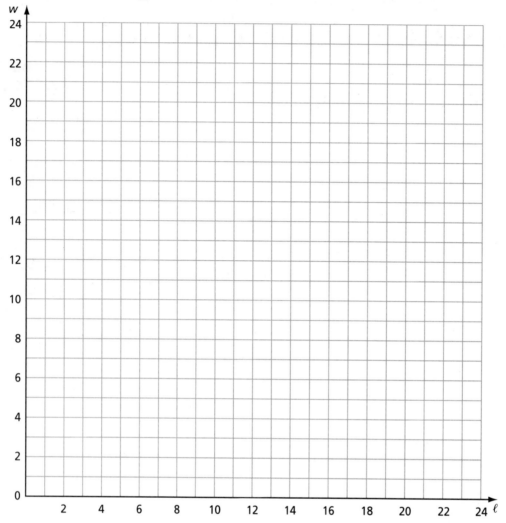

ℓ	w
1	
2	

ℓ	w
1	
2	

Name _____

NUMBER AND OPERATIONS

Complete the table of values. Then graph the function. ◄1. MOC 077, 251–252

1. $y = x^2$

x	y
−3	
−2	
−1	
0	
1	
2	
3	

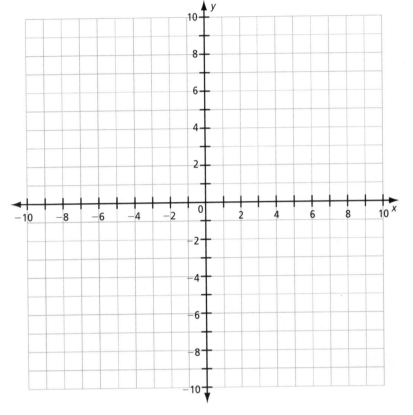

Use your graph from problem 1 to solve. ◄2–4. MOC 077, 251–252

2. Describe the shape of the graph of an equation that contains a square of a variable.

_____

3. Find 5 on the y-axis. What is the value of x on your graph?

_____

4. What does that tell you about the square roots of 5?

_____

PATTERNS AND ALGEBRA

Show your work. ◄5. MOC 205–206

5. Use substitution to find an equivalent equation with y as its only variable. Then, solve for y. $y − x = 5$ and $2y + x = 19$

GEOMETRY AND MEASUREMENT

Draw the shape. ◂6. MOC 404–415

6. Complete the drawing of a figure that has a square base, 5 vertices, 8 edges, and 5 faces. What is the name of the shape you have drawn?

_____

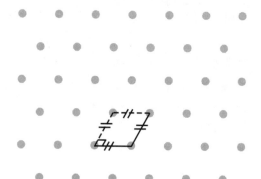

Solve. ◂7. MOC 365–366

7. Label the dimensions of the rectangle. Show your work.

$P = 20$
$A = 24$ w _____

ℓ _____

REVIEW

Write the value of each expression. ◂8–21. MOC 164, 193, 209

8. $-2 \times (-2)$ _____

9. $4 \times (-2)$ _____

10. $-2 \div (-2)$ _____

11. $4 \div (-2)$ _____

12. $-2 + (-2) \times (-3)$ _____

13. $12 \div 3 \times (-2)$ _____

14. $2 + (-2)$ _____

15. $-2 + (-2) + (-2)$ _____

16. $-2 + 4 \times 5$ _____

17. $15 - (-6)$ _____

18. $-15 - (-6)$ _____

19. $-2 - 6 \times (-2)$ _____

20. $-2 + 6 \div (-3)$ _____

21. $(-2 + 6) \div (-3)$ _____

GLOSSARY TO GO

Review the definitions and illustrations you added to your Glossary this week. Make additions or corrections if you need to.

Problem Solving: Products and Sums

DIRECTIONS

- Solve the problem. Circle the strategies you used.
- Show your work.

PROBLEM 1

Two whole numbers have a sum of 10 and a product of 24. What are the numbers?

_____

PROBLEM 2

Two whole numbers have a sum of 17 and a product of 60. What are the numbers?

_____

ANALYZE YOUR WORK

1. Did your work on the first problem help you with the second problem? If so, how?

_____

_____

2. Write and graph equations for Problem 1 on page 148. Why do the graphs intersect twice?

_____

_____

Problem Solving: Products and Sums

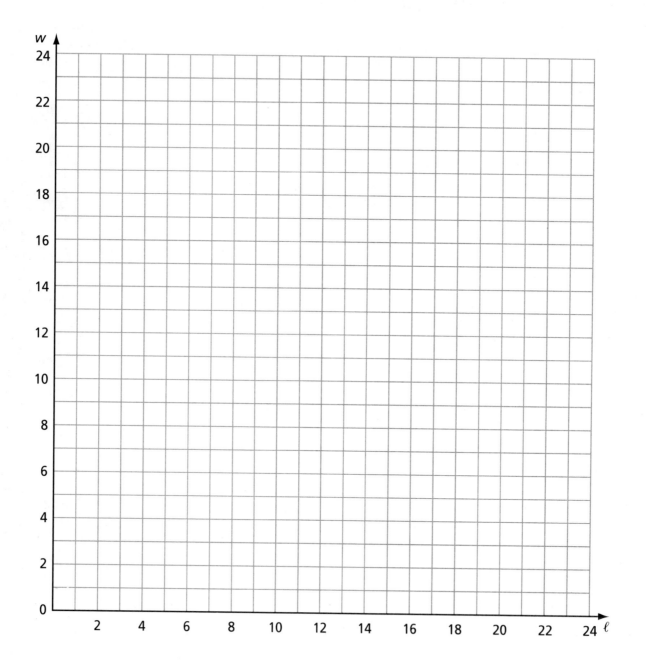

NEWSLETTER

Summer Success: Math

This week, your child has been working with scientific notation, positive and negative fractions, volume and surface area, and probability.

Probability is a tricky concept. You hear it used every day when the weather reporter announces the chance of rain tomorrow. The important thing to know about probability is that it doesn't ever say what must happen, only what is likely to happen. So, just as it may not rain in your neighborhood when the report says there's a 75% chance of precipitation, a coin may not land tails-up exactly half of the time.

On the back of this page is a probability experiment to try with your child. If you have a dime and a quarter, there are four ways they can land.

Dime	Quarter
heads	heads
heads	tails
tails	tails
tails	heads

From this chart, you can see that the probability is that the coins will land different-sides up half of the time.

 Enjoy your time with your child, and thank you for helping to strengthen your child's comfort with important math concepts.

Probability Experiment

- Flip 2 coins 20 times and write the combinations of heads and tails that appear each time.

Two Heads	Two Tails	One Head, One Tail

- Which combination appeared most often—2 heads, 2 tails, or one of each?

- Why do you think that might be so?

It might be interesting to work with your child to repeat this experiment several times. Perhaps your results will be closer to the probability if you do many trials.

Enjoy these activities with your child. Remember that using math in the real world helps your child understand that math is important in school.

GLOSSARY TO GO

central angle

concave polygon

circumference

coordinate grid

common multiple

cylinder

degree

E

equation

F

factors

fraction

integer

_____

I J K

L M

order of operations

ordered pair

P

percent

_____

_____

_____

_____

_____

polyhedron (polyhedra)

_____

_____

_____

_____

_____

_____

pyramid

_____

_____

_____

_____

_____

_____

Q

R

ratio

regular polygon

repeating decimal

scientific notation

similar polygons

supplementary angles

surface area

volume

Name _____

NUMBER

Choose the best answer or write a response for each question.

1. What is another way to write $\frac{1}{5}$ as a percent?

   Ⓐ 20%

   Ⓑ 2%

   Ⓒ 0.2%

   Ⓓ 2.0%

2. Write $\frac{1}{6}$ as a decimal.

   Ⓐ 0.16

   Ⓑ $0.1\overline{6}$

   Ⓒ 0.17

   Ⓓ $0.\overline{6}$

3. What is the opposite of −9?

   Ⓐ −9

   Ⓑ 8

   Ⓒ 9

   Ⓓ 10

4. What is the prime factorization of 32?

   Ⓐ 8×4

   Ⓑ $2 \times 2 \times 2 \times 2 \times 2$

   Ⓒ $2 \times 2 \times 2 \times 4$

   Ⓓ $8 \times 2 \times 2$

5. Fill in the table of values for $x + y = 8$.

x	y
0	
1	
2	
3	

6. Which number does **not** have the same value as the others?

   Ⓐ $5.7 + 10^6$

   Ⓑ 5,700,000

   Ⓒ 5.7×10^6

   Ⓓ 5 million, 700 thousand

OPERATIONS

7. What is $\frac{1}{2}$ of $\frac{1}{2}$?

- (A) $1\frac{1}{2}$
- (B) 1
- (C) $\frac{1}{2}$
- (D) $\frac{1}{4}$

8. What is $\frac{3}{4} - \frac{1}{2}$?

- (A) $1\frac{1}{2}$
- (B) 1
- (C) $\frac{1}{2}$
- (D) $\frac{1}{4}$

9. Select the number line that shows the expression:

$$-3 - (-3)$$

- (A)
  -6 -5 -4 -3 -2 -1 0 1
- (B)
  -6 -5 -4 -3 -2 -1 0 1
- (C)
  -6 -5 -4 -3 -2 -1 0 1
- (D)
  -6 -5 -4 -3 -2 -1 0 1

10. What is the value of $2^3 \times 2$?

- (A) 6
- (B) 12
- (C) 16
- (D) 36

11. What is the value of x if $4x + 2 = 8$?

- (A) 34
- (B) 2
- (C) $1\frac{1}{2}$
- (D) 1

12. What is $-\frac{1}{2} \times \frac{1}{3}$?

- (A) $-\frac{1}{3}$
- (B) $-\frac{1}{6}$
- (C) $\frac{2}{6}$
- (D) $\frac{2}{3}$

PATTERNS AND ALGEBRA

13. Continue the pattern.

0.5, 1.0, 1.5, 2.0, 2.5, _____,

_____, _____

14. What is the value of term 8 for this pattern?

0.125, 0.25, 0.375, 0.5, ...

- (A) 0.625
- (B) 0.75
- (C) 0.875
- (D) 1

15. What is the value of the expression?

$$-5 \times 9 \times (-1) \times (-1)$$

- (A) 45
- (B) −45
- (C) 2
- (D) not given

16. Continue the pattern.

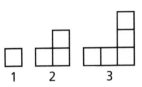

1   2   3   4

Find the area of the first 4 figures.

Figure	Area
1	
2	
3	
4	

17. If $4a = 2.8$ and $a + b = 1.5$, what is the value of b?

- (A) 1.5
- (B) 1
- (C) 0.8
- (D) 0.7

18. One circle weighs as much as how many triangles?

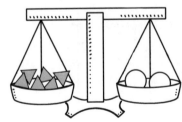

- (A) 6
- (B) 4
- (C) 3
- (D) 2

GEOMETRY AND MEASUREMENT

19. Which regular polygon has 3 lines of symmetry?

Ⓐ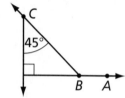

Ⓑ

Ⓒ

Ⓓ

20. What is the measure of angle *ABC*?

Ⓐ 45°

Ⓑ 90°

Ⓒ 135°

Ⓓ 180°

21. Plot the points and connect them in order.
$(-2, 3), (2, 3), (0, -3), (-4, -3), (-2, 3)$

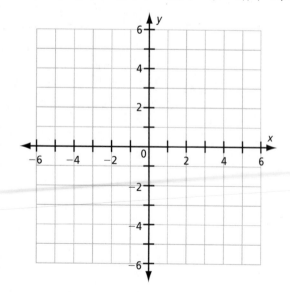

22. Which diagram shows a polygon with central angles?

Ⓐ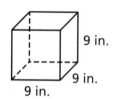

Ⓑ

Ⓒ

Ⓓ

Use the cube to answer problems 23–24.

9 in.

9 in.

9 in.

23. Find the surface area of the cube.

Ⓐ 22 in.²

Ⓑ 81 in.²

Ⓒ 486 in.²

Ⓓ 729 in.²

24. Find the volume of the cube.

Ⓐ 27 in.³

Ⓑ 81 in.³

Ⓒ 486 in.³

Ⓓ 729 in.³

DATA

Use the data for problems 25–27.

Unpopped Popcorn Sales in the United States

Year	Pounds Sold (millions)
1975	390
1980	570
1985	670
1990	940
1995	1,000
2000	980

Source: popcorn.org

25. Make a scatter plot.

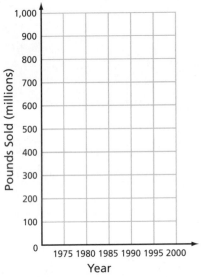

26. Do you see a trend in the data?

_____

27. Make a stem-and-leaf plot.

Popcorn Sales

Stems	Leaves

Key _____

You have 5 red and 5 blue counters in a bag. You pick a counter and return it to the bag. Use the data for problems 28–30.

Tally	
Red	卌 卌 卌 卌 Ⅲ
Blue	卌 卌 卌

28. Which circle graph **best** represents the results of the experiment?

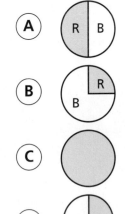

29. Explain why a bar graph would also be appropriate to display the experimental results.

_____

_____

_____

30. What is the theoretical probability of picking red?

(A) $\frac{2}{1}$

(B) $\frac{23}{15}$

(C) $\frac{15}{23}$

(D) $\frac{1}{2}$

PROBLEM SOLVING

Show your work.

31. Together, Mia and Cia have $33. Cia has $\frac{3}{8}$ as much money as Mia does.

How much does Mia have? _____

How much does Cia have? _____

32. In the following equations, each letter stands for a **different** integer.
What integer does each letter stand for?

$a + b = b$

$b + b = -10$

$a - c = 3$

$a =$ _____

$b =$ _____

$c =$ _____